THE KEW GARDENER'S GUIDE TO

GROWING
BULBS

Royal Botanic Gardens Kew

THE KEW GARDENER'S GUIDE TO

GROWING BULBS

THE ART AND SCIENCE TO
GROW YOUR OWN BULBS

RICHARD WILFORD

WHITE LION
PUBLISHING

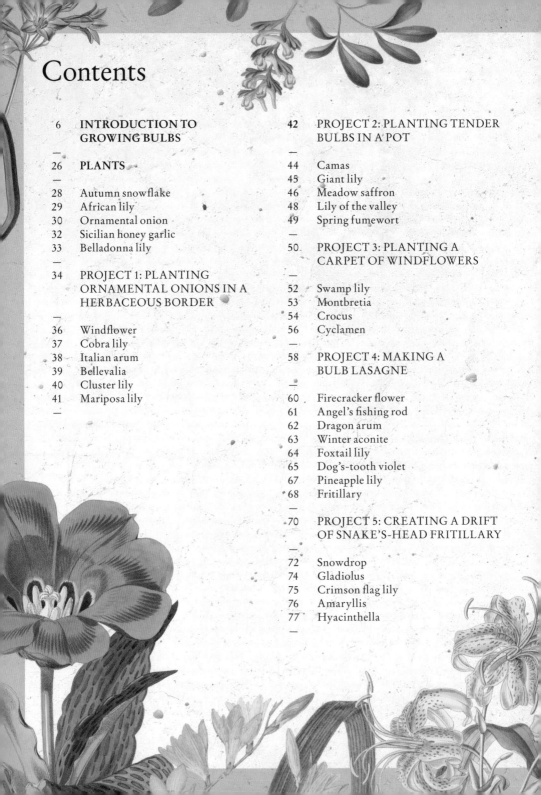

Contents

Introduction to growing bulbs

—

THE VALUE OF BULBS

Bulbs are easy, colourful, diverse and beautiful garden plants. Whether you have a large country garden or a window box, there will be a bulb that you can grow.

Although best known for their spring flowers, there are bulbs for every month of the year, from the depths of winter to the height of summer. When you plant a bulb in autumn it could be flowering in three or four months, while a bulb planted in late summer could be flowering in just a few weeks. What easier and quicker way is there to transform your garden?

The word 'bulb' is used for a range of different plants, but the one thing they have in common is a dormant period, when they survive underground. Plants have many ways of surviving tough conditions in their natural habitat and, if they live somewhere that is seasonally dry, then retreating underground is one way to make it through a long period of drought. Bulbs do this by storing all the food they need to re-grow in a neat package. This is what makes them so easy to plant. You buy a dry bulb, bury it in the garden and bring it back to life with water.

There is a little more to it than that, of course. Bulbs need light – sometimes lots of it – and when they are dormant they usually do not want to be too wet. Some bulbs put up with almost anything, and others die at a mere sniff of water at the wrong time. The bulbs that are commonly sold and easy to find are mostly very easy to grow. Daffodils (*Narcissus*), tulips, hyacinths, crocuses and ornamental onions (*Allium*) are all reliable garden plants.

Throughout this book I use the word 'bulb' to describe any plant that has an underground food-storage organ, technically called a geophyte, which literally means 'earth plant'. But plants have different ways of storing food. As well as true bulbs there are corms, tubers and rhizomes, all performing basically the same function. So what is a true bulb?

OPPOSITE *Tulipa* 'Red Shine' brings early colour to a herbaceous border.

Gladioli, such as this beautiful *Gladiolus* × *byzantinus*, grow from corms but behave in the same way as true bulbs.

TRUE BULBS

A true bulb stores food for the next season in swollen leaf bases. As a leaf dies back, the base, which is underground, swells with moisture and food. Every year a new stem and leaves grow from a bud at the very centre of the bulb, and new roots grow from the base. Over time, the leaf bases form layers in the bulb, the youngest at the centre. Cut a bulb in half and you will see the layers. An onion (*Allium*) is a good example of a bulb with clearly visible layers. As the layers are pushed outwards, they become thinner and are often enclosed by a crispy, outer layer called a bulb tunic. Over the years, a true bulb will get bigger and bigger.

There are exceptions, such as tulips, in which all the bulb's food is used up when the plant grows and a new bulb forms to replace it. These bulbs do not have the layers that build up over time, but they still have the bulb tunic, which can be quite thick and leathery in some species and may help insulate the bulb from freezing conditions. Other plants such as lilies do not have bulbs with layers; instead, the leaf bases form scales that are loose except where they join at the base. They also lack the tunic. Garlic is a bulb, but the leaf bases form the cloves. These are all bulbs because they are formed from the leaves, but other geophytes store food in different parts of the plant.

CORMS

A corm can be grown just like a true bulb, but it is formed from a swollen stem. The leaves die back completely, but the part of the stem that is underground swells up and stores the food for the new growth. There are no layers as in a bulb; a corm is solid and can be quite hard. There are buds at the top that will grow into a new stem and leaves, and roots develop from the base. A corm is usually renewed every year, because all the food is used up by the plant when it grows. It generally has a dry outer layer, like a bulb, and if you dig one up you often find the dry remains of the old corm beneath the new one.

A crocus is a corm, as are gladioli, montbretias (*Crocosmia*) and meadow saffron (*Colchicum*). Bulbs and corms are very similar when it comes to growing them. The only thing to bear in mind is that, because a corm is renewed every year, it is important that the plant gets enough light and moisture when it is growing to make a strong, healthy new corm.

TUBERS

A tuber can be a swollen stem or root. It grows underground and stores food just like a bulb or corm. Examples include cyclamen, cobra lilies (*Arisaema*), arums, spring fumeworts (*Corydalis solida*) and winter aconites (*Eranthis hyemalis*).

A stem tuber has buds on its surface that grow into new stems and leaves, and roots normally grow from the base. There can be more than one bud. If you look at an old cyclamen tuber, for example, you can see several buds on the top surface, sometimes forming little, woody growths from which the new flowers and leaves arise. Root tubers such as foxtail lilies (*Eremurus*) are modified roots and form buds only where they are attached to the stem.

Most tubers can be grown just like bulbs, although some, such as cyclamen, need to be planted near the soil surface instead of being buried in the ground.

RHIZOMES

A rhizome is an underground stem that is often horizontal and creeping. It has buds that give rise to new leaves, stems and roots. Rhizomes are common in plants that die down for part of the year, such as herbaceous perennials, but they can be swollen to store nutrients. Not all rhizomatous plants are drought tolerant; they may die down to escape the cold and short days of winter. Those that have fleshy rhizomes are adapted to seasonal droughts, and they include many plants that can be grown in a similar way to bulbs.

Drought-tolerant rhizomatous plants include the African lily (*Agapanthus*) and crimson flag lily (*Hesperantha coccinea*). Some rhizomes are not especially adapted to dry conditions, but are sold alongside bulbs, and they are dormant for the drier time of year. These include the wake robin (*Trillium*) and lily of the valley (*Convallaria majalis*).

When buying lily bulbs, look out for healthy ones that have not dried out too much and do not have mould growing on them.

Snowdrops can be bought 'in the green', when they are still in growth, but you must plant them straightaway.

CHOOSING AND BUYING BULBS

Summer is when the catalogues arrive. These will be full of winter- and spring-flowering bulbs, and a few autumn ones such as meadow saffron (*Colchicum*). Such bulbs are all summer dormant so this is when they are sold and they will soon need planting. Garden centres and plant nurseries will display bulbs on their shelves, with colourful packaging to tempt you. Summer-flowering bulbs are sold in winter and spring, for spring planting.

Whether looking through colourful catalogues or browsing web pages, choosing the bulbs to buy can be a daunting task, so here is some advice. If you want to plant bulbs in your garden, buy fewer varieties in larger numbers, rather than a few bulbs of many varieties. A drift of 25–50 tulips, for example, looks far more impressive than a patch of five.

Also think about flowering time.

You could plant an early bulb such as *Narcissus* 'February Gold' to kick-start the season or you might prefer a full-on spring extravaganza with all your bulbs flowering at the same time.

If you are planting up containers, then fewer bulbs is fine. Ten tulips in a pot is plenty and different pots can have different bulbs. You can plant more than one variety in each pot, layering the bulbs like a lasagne (see page 58) and creating wonderful colour combinations.

You do not have to buy bulbs when they are dormant. Flowering bulbs can be purchased in pots for an instant display. Once they have finished flowering, make sure you plant them in the garden, where they should flower again the following year. Buying snowdrops (*Galanthus*) 'in the green', after flowering but still in leaf, is fairly common practice now and you can purchase trays of newly dug up bulbs ready for immediate planting.

Although it is best to plant bulbs as soon as you get them, some such as tulips can be left until late autumn.

When buying bulbs from a shop or garden centre, look out for plump, firm ones. Avoid them if they are very soft, have rotten patches or mould on the surface. The earlier you get them, the healthier they are likely to be. You can pick up some great cut-price bargains late in the bulb buying season, but they often do not like sitting on the shelves for weeks or months, as they can dry out too much, although some such as tulips and ornamental onions (*Allium*) can withstand this treatment better than others. Also, look out for bulbs that have started into growth while still in their packets. They need planting at once. This is especially true of meadow saffron (*Colchicum*), which can flower in the garden in early autumn and might try to do so while still in the shop.

If you buy your bulbs online then try and use a reputable supplier. Word of mouth is a good guide, and there will be online reviews to read. Be wary of bulbs that seem very cheap. If you are buying large quantities, like a bag of daffodils, then they will be a good price, but bulbs are graded by suppliers and smaller ones are generally cheaper. They might not flower in their first year or they may be weak growers that may not survive.

BULBS IN THE GARDEN

Winter

In the middle of winter, with frosty mornings and maybe a covering of snow, there seems little life in the garden, but look carefully and you see snowdrops (*Galanthus*) poking through the icy ground. Under trees you might find yellow blooms of winter aconite (*Eranthis hyemalis*) or pink *Cyclamen coum*, and then the first crocuses appear.

Against the bare soil it is easy for winter bulbs to make a show, and by the time spring and summer plants are growing they will have safely disappeared underground. If you do not want to brave the weather, plant them so you can see them from your window or grow them in pots by your door. Of all the bulbs you can plant, it is these winter flowers that bring the most hope.

Spring

If winter bulbs bring hope, then spring ones provide the joy you were hoping for. Once the weather warms, bulbs start to grow quickly. New shoots soon elongate and in a short time they flower, transforming your garden. Spring is the season of daffodils (*Narcissus*), tulips, hyacinths and fritillaries, but there are so many more to grow.

In early spring, crocuses decorate the grass with their jewel-like blooms. Under deciduous trees, dog's-tooth violets (*Erythronium*), blue squills (*Scilla*) or a carpet of anemones will all flower under the bare branches before the trees grow their leaves.

In a garden border, spring bulbs fill the gaps between shrubs and flower as herbaceous perennials are just waking up. They complement other spring flowers such as forget-me-nots (*Myosotis*) and bleeding heart (*Lamprocapnos spectabilis*). Grow daffodils with Siberian bugloss (*Brunnera*), and tulips with the fresh young leaves of lupins. The season ends with bluebells (*Hyacinthoides*) in an increasingly shady woodland and tall camas (*Camassia*) flowering among the lengthening grass.

Summer

Summer bulbs have to compete in a garden at its floral peak. The season starts with the tall, ornamental drumstick onions (*Allium*), their purple flower heads appearing above quickly growing herbaceous perennials in a border. These ornamental onions are really late-flowering spring bulbs, blooming at the end of their growing season.

Montbretia (*Crocosmia*) has fantastic, lance-shaped leaves that form dense clumps from which the flower spikes arise. The flowers are the brightly coloured highlights, but the leaves remain right through till autumn. Lilies (*Lilium*) flower at the tops of their leafy stems. These leaves may be held in whorls, as in the martagon lily (*L. martagon*), which flowers in early summer. Later lilies, such as *L. henryi*, can bloom on lofty stems that hold the flowers high above the surrounding plants.

At a lower level, the smaller pineapple lilies (*Eucomis*) and later-flowering ornamental onions such as *Allium senescens* will not compete with taller plants, but need some space of their own. They can be used to fill a gap left by early-summer perennials such as oriental poppies (*Papaver orientale*). It is

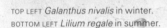

TOP LEFT *Galanthus nivalis* in winter.
BOTTOM LEFT *Lilium regale* in summer.

TOP RIGHT *Narcissus pseudonarcissus* in spring.
BOTTOM RIGHT *Colchicum autumnale* in autumn.

more important than in other seasons to understand the relationship between bulbs and the rest of the garden, if you are going to make best use of summer bulbs in your borders.

Autumn

Bulbs that have their dormant season in summer will begin to grow in autumn. This coincides with the arrival of rain in their natural habitat, breaking the drought. For most, root growth starts first and then the leaves appear, followed by the flowers in spring. But some flower first, before their leaves grow, and these can give the garden a lift as the glories of summer begin to fade.

One of the joys of autumn bulbs is that they seem to appear suddenly from nowhere. One minute the soil is bare and the next it is dotted with colourful blooms. Autumn-flowering crocuses such as *C. speciosus* and *C. nudiflorus*, produce goblet-shaped blooms in early autumn, in a lawn or at the base of a tree. Meadow saffron (*Colchicum*) is similar and often misleadingly called autumn crocus, but the flowers are larger and their leaves wider.

The first flowers of the ivy-leaved cyclamen (*Cyclamen hederifolium*) can open in late summer, soon followed by autumn snowflake (*Acis autumnalis*). The pink trumpets of nerines and belladonna lily (*Amaryllis belladonna*) are autumn blooms and are among the taller bulbs flowering at this time of year.

Naturalizing bulbs

One very effective way to grow bulbs in your garden is to naturalize them. This means planting so they appear to have naturally colonized an area; then they will spread themselves through a border or a lawn once established. (See also Seeing bulbs in the wild, page 133.) Spring bulbs are the most effective for this type of planting but some autumn bulbs work well too.

The most important aspect of planting bulbs in this way is to arrange them in a random pattern. Do not space them out evenly because the result will look too artificial. Take a handful of bulbs and throw them on the ground. Plant them where they land. Some may end up close together, but as long as they are not touching and there is at least a bulb's width between them they will be fine. You may end up with small areas with no bulbs at all but that does not matter. The idea is to create the look of a natural drift of plants, thicker in some places, with empty spaces between.

Naturalizing bulbs is the best way to grow them in a lawn. Randomly scatter the bulbs and dig individual holes for each one with a trowel or bulb planter, at least three times the depth of the bulb. Daffodils (*Narcissus*) can be planted this way; there are many that look great in a lawn, from the low-growing *N. bulbocodium* to the taller *N. pseudonarcissus*. Later flowering is the poeticus daffodil or pheasant's eye (*N. poeticus*). A tall bulb that does well in grass is camas (*Camassia leichtlinii*). You will have to leave cutting the grass until after the leaves have died back

so this type of planting is not for a formal area. Camas and the poeticus daffodil both flower in late spring so the grass will have to stay long until early summer.

Small bulbs for naturalizing include snowdrops (*Galanthus*), crocuses (both spring and autumn forms), squills (*Scilla*) and the snake's-head fritillary (*Fritillaria meleagris*). To plant these in grass, you could lift some of the turf, place the bulbs in a random pattern on the exposed soil and roll back the grass to cover them. Some bulbs, such as snake's-head fritillary and *Narcissus bulbocodium*, need some moisture year-round so plant them in a damper part of the lawn if you can.

Of course, you can naturalize these same bulbs in a border, and this is also the best way to establish colonies of winter aconite (*Eranthis hyemalis*), spring anemones such as Grecian windflower (*Anemone blanda*), dog's-tooth violet (*Erythronium*), meadow saffron (*Colchicum*) and bright red *Tulipa sprengeri*. And in a border, you do not need to worry about when you cut the grass.

After flowering

The flowers of bulbs are their main attraction but what you do with them after flowering is important for their long-term survival. The plant must build up enough food resources for it to survive the dormant season and be able to grow again. This food is produced by the leaves so removing them too early will have an impact on the strength of the bulb. Leaves of

Autumn-flowering *Crocus speciosus* naturalizes well in grass.

Once the bulb's leaves have gone brown and dry, they can easily be pulled away. If there is any resistance, leave them a little longer. Leaving the decaying leaves on the ground can lead to fungal infections that might spread to the bulb so it is worthwhile removing them. The flower stem may last longer, especially if they are holding seed pods, but there is no harm in cutting them back early, unless you want the seeds.

Ornamental onions (*Allium*) flower at the end of their growing season and often the leaves have already died back when they bloom. The seed heads of many ornamental onions are attractive so can be left to decorate the garden, but eventually they will begin to deteriorate and become untidy and you can cut them off at ground level.

If you garden on damp, heavy soil and you are worried that your bulbs may not survive the summer, you can lift the bulbs once they have finished flowering. When the leaves show signs of going brown, it is safe to dig them up. Do not remove the leaves but allow them to die back naturally. Then the bulbs can be stored somewhere cool, dry and dark, such as a garden shed or garage, until autumn when you can replant them. This method is often used for tulip cultivars, as they resent too much summer moisture. It also allows the bulbs to be sorted by size so you replant the largest ones back in the garden and discard the smaller ones or grow them on to flowering size in a corner of the garden. You can also lift half-hardy summer bulbs that will not survive winter in the ground.

bulbs planted in the garden should be allowed to die back naturally. Tying them up to make them look neat will reduce their ability to photosynthesize and weaken the bulb.

If the bulbs are growing in grass, you should leave the grass to grow until the bulbs have died back. Early bulbs such as snowdrops and spring crocuses will die back before the grass is getting too untidy. Growing daffodils in grass, especially the later-flowering varieties, will mean allowing the grass to grow long before you can cut it. A general rule is that the grass should be left for six weeks after the bulbs have flowered.

SOIL PREPARATION AND PLANTING

Good soil is the key to a successful garden. It is worth preparing the soil before planting, to give your plants the best start. They require water, air and nutrients, and most bulbs need good drainage. Soil that is moisture-retentive but well-drained might sound like a contradiction but it is the perfect soil for many bulbs. It means that the soil does not dry out quickly but holds some moisture for the plants to take up, while allowing excess water to drain away. Very few bulbs will survive sitting in waterlogged soil when they are dormant. They are adapted to survive a drought during their dormant season, when very little water is available, and sitting in wet ground can result in the bulb rotting away.

Soil is made up of three main components: sand, silt and clay. Sand has the largest particles and clay the smallest. Soil made up of predominantly clay particles will be dense and sticky, as anyone who gardens on clay will know very well, and when it dries out it becomes very hard. It is the worst soil for bulbs. Sandy soil is light and airy but lacks nutrients and water drains quickly. This is fine when the bulbs are dormant but they will struggle to get enough moisture when in growth. The perfect soil, often called loam, has roughly equal parts sand and silt and a smaller proportion of clay. It will also have organic matter from decaying plant material, which adds extra nutrients.

To improve your soil, add organic matter such as decomposed garden compost, leafmould and well-rotted manure. In heavy clay soil, this will open up the texture, allowing air in and water to move through it. This will not happen instantly, and it can take several years to turn heavy clay soil into a good loamy mix by adding organic matter every year. In sandy soil, the organic matter will help retain some moisture and also provide more nutrients for the plants. A sandy soil is better for bulbs than clay soil, but they may need extra nutrients to keep them healthy. This can be provided by adding a low-nitrogen fertilizer to the soil, such as blood, fish and bone or diluted tomato feed, when the bulbs are in growth.

Soils also vary in their pH. Acid soils have a low pH and alkaline soils a high pH, with neutral soil in between and having a pH of around seven. You can buy a soil testing kit to find out the pH of your soil. Most bulbs are fine in neutral to slightly alkaline soil and will tolerate some acidity. Few bulbs need acid soil – the main exception being the oriental lily hybrids. A general rule is that woodland bulbs, such as dog's-tooth violets (*Erythronium*), wake robin (*Trillium*) and *Narcissus cyclamineus*, are more likely to tolerate acid soils.

Once you have prepared your soil, it is time to plant your bulbs. Planting depth will depend on the size of the bulb: the larger the bulb, the deeper the hole. For most small bulbs, a planting depth of 10cm/4in is recommended. For larger bulbs, dig a hole with a depth at least three times the size of the bulb. So for a bulb that is 5cm/2in from top to bottom the hole should be at least 15cm/6in deep. The top layer of soil can dry out on a mild day, and bulbs planted in this layer can suffer from too little moisture when they are in growth. If planted too shallow, larger bulbs such as tulips can split into smaller bulbs that will not flower.

There are exceptions, and if a bulb needs shallow planting it is mentioned under the individual entries in this book (see pages 26–132). Cyclamen, for example, need to be planted near the surface as their flower stems cannot push through a thick soil layer. But for most bulbs, deeper planting is better.

OPPOSITE TOP Good garden soil is a mixture of sand, silt and clay, with organic matter.
OPPOSITE MIDDLE Well-prepared soil is easy to dig with a trowel when planting bulbs.
OPPOSITE BELOW A simple range of tools is all you need for growing bulbs: a spade, trowel or bulb planter for digging holes; a pot for small bulbs; and grit to mulch the soil.

GROWING BULBS IN POTS

Growing bulbs in containers liberates you from the constraints of your garden soil. It also allows you to move plants around easily and protect them from cold and wet weather, and if you do not have a garden you can grow bulbs in a window box or planter on your doorstep. You can try out different combinations of bulbs by mixing them in one container and, when the spring bulbs have finished, swap them for summer or autumn bulbs.

Choose a container that will be in scale with the bulbs you are growing when they are in flower. Tall lilies and the large tulips, for example, need a large, deep pot but smaller bulbs can be grown in wide, relatively shallow pans, window boxes or small terracotta pots. Smaller pots will dry out more quickly so be sure to regularly check the soil moisture level when the bulbs are growing. A large pot is easy to overwater; the soil may feel dry near the surface but lower down it can still be wet, so dig down a little when checking for watering needs. It is essential the pot has holes in the bottom to allow water to drain away.

The soil in the pot should be a good-quality loam-based mix and to that you can add some gravel to ensure it drains well. Mix two parts loam-based soil with one part of 3–5mm gravel for most bulbs. Woodland species could have leafmould or other organic matter added, instead of grit. This will also aid drainage, but retains more moisture and is ideal for plants that prefer humus-rich soil.

When planting, fill the pot to about two-thirds of its depth with soil mix. Plant the bulbs on the soil surface,

Small bulbs such as this *Hyacinthella dalmatica* are perfect for growing in pots, as are grape hyacinths (*Muscari*).

evenly spaced and not touching. (Bulbs that need very well-drained soil can be planted on a layer of sharp sand to protect the base of each bulb from dampness when they are dormant.) Then fill the pot, to within 2.5cm/1in of its rim, with more of the soil mix. Finally, you can cover the surface with a layer of gravel. Apart from looking good, this protects the plant's leaves from soil splashing on to them when it rains or when watering the pot.

After planting, water the pot thoroughly. When water starts pouring out of the base of the pot you know the soil is wet through. Until the leaves start to appear above soil level, water

Choose a container that suits the bulb and will be sturdy enough for its top growth.

This attractive terracotta pan is deep enough for a bulb such as this cyclamen, which does not require deep planting.

the pot only occasionally, when the soil is starting to feel dry. When growth is well underway, the soil should be kept moist. Also, if you are planning to keep the bulbs for another year, it is well worth giving them a liquid feed every couple of weeks while they are growing. Use a low-nitrogen feed such as tomato food diluted to half strength, which will help the bulb build up strength but not encourage too much leafy growth.

Once the bulbs have finished flowering you should still water the pots while the leaves are green; as soon as they start to brown, reduce watering significantly. Then you can move the pot somewhere dry to give the bulbs their

rest. This can be under a greenhouse bench, under some trees or the eaves of your house. If you want to reuse the container straight away, you will have to tip out the bulbs and dry them off out of the soil. You can plant the bulbs in the garden and use new ones for the display next year.

If you do not have a garden, try growing bulbs in a window box. Suitable bulbs include crocuses, reticulate irises, hyacinths, smaller daffodils such as *Narcissus* 'Tête-à-tête', 'Hawera' and 'Jack Snipe' and grape hyacinths (*Muscari*). Or you can fill the window box with tulips, for a one-off spectacular display.

SIMPLE PROPAGATION

If you would like more bulbs but do not want to keep buying them, there are some simple ways to propagate the bulbs you have. A healthy plant naturally increases over time, and sometimes when you buy a bulb it has smaller offsets alongside the main bulb. You often see this in daffodils (*Narcissus*). These offsets grow into full-sized bulbs in a year or two and gradually a clump will form with several bulbs growing together, all producing a flower stem. The easiest way to increase the number of bulbs you have is by division.

Bulb division

Bulbs should be divided when they are dormant, although snowdrops (*Galanthus*) and winter aconites (*Eranthis hyemalis*) can be separated when in growth. For the rest, you can lift them once the leaves have almost completely died back. If the leaves have already disappeared you will have to dig around to locate the bulbs, unless you have marked the spot.

Dig up the whole clump and tease it apart until you have separated out the individual bulbs. These can then be replanted, spreading them out so the size of the colony is increased, or you can start a new patch in a new location. As you separate the bulbs, you will often see they have produced offsets that are still attached to the main bulb. This is most commonly seen in true bulbs – less so in corms and tubers (see page 10). Carefully pull the offsets away

The simplest way to increase your bulbs such as snowdrops here is to pull away offsets from the main bulb and grow them on separately.

and replant along with the main bulbs. The extra space each bulb gains will encourage further offsets to grow.

If you have grown the bulbs in a pot, tip them out after they have died down completely. Retrieve the bulbs from the dry soil and separate the main bulbs from any offsets that have developed. The larger bulbs, which should flower again, can be stored cool and dry while dormant and then used to plant up a new container. The smaller offsets can be potted separately and grown on to flowering size or be planted out in the garden.

Tiny new bulbs, called cormlets, bulblets or bulbils, can form around the base of the parent bulb, at the base of the stem or occasionally (most often in lilies) in the leaf axils above ground. These need more care when growing on, as they are so small. Plant them in a site that does not get too hot and dry, or plant them in a pot that you regularly check for moisture. The soil should not be allowed to dry out completely.

Scoring, scaling and chipping

With true bulbs, the production of bulblets can be induced by scoring or by cutting the bulb into pieces. The layers of a bulb are joined at the basal plate, that is, the roughly circular bottom of the bulb from which the roots grow. The basal plate has a vital role in the production of bulblets.

Scoring involves cutting a shallow cross in the basal plate but keeping the bulb intact. This is done towards the end of the bulb's dormant season and you should use a sharp, sterile knife. After making the cuts, place the bulb upright in a tray of sand so the basal plate is covered. Keep the sand slightly moist by spraying with water daily, but make sure it is never very wet. New bulblets will form along the cuts made in the basal plate, in a few weeks. When they are large enough to handle, pick them off and plant them in a pot of soil mix (see Growing bulbs in pots, page 20). The soil should be kept fairly moist so the bulblets do not dry out. They will grow leaves at the same time as the parent bulb would normally come into growth; slowly the bulblets will increase in size. When they go dormant, tip them out of the pot and plant in a larger pot or in the garden.

Some bulbs such as lilies have loose scales, and these can be pulled away from the bulb and grown into new bulbs. This is called scaling. Carefully detach a few scales from the parent bulb, towards the end of its growing season. Place the scales in a plastic bag of moist vermiculite and keep in a warm room. In a few weeks each scale will grow a small bulblet. When the bulblet has formed roots, transfer it to a pot of soil mix and grow it on.

For bulbs with regular layers, such as daffodils (*Narcissus*), hyacinths, snowdrops (*Galanthus*) and squills (*Scilla*), bulblets can be grown by cutting a dormant bulb into pieces, but it is essential for each piece to include a portion of basal plate. Cut the bulb vertically into wedge-shaped sections, or 'chips', each with part of the basal plate. The chips should be treated in the same way as scales, and they will grow bulblets from the portion of basal plate. If you are feeling adventurous, a more intricate method, called twin-scaling, is to cut the bulb into small pieces, each with two segments of bulb layer, or 'scales', attached by a tiny portion of the basal plate. Twin-scaling can result in more bulblets than chipping.

The new bulbs obtained by division, scoring, chipping and scaling will all be identical to the parent plant. These methods are used to propagate bulbs that do not produce viable seed, such as many tulip and daffodil cultivars.

Sowing seed
Growing a flowering bulb from seed can take several years but you can get many more bulbs this way than from vegetative propagation.

After flowering, look out for the seed pods. Some bulbs such as ornamental onions (*Allium*) make attractive seed heads held well above the ground, while others such as crocuses keep their seed pods at ground level and you will have to search around for them among the dying leaves. As the seed pod goes brown it will start to split open, and this is the time to harvest the seed by cutting off the seed pod and opening it up or by placing it in a paper bag to catch the seed as it falls out (see Growing bulbs from seed, page 104). The seeds may be small, round and black (like tiny peppercorns) or be large, flat and papery.

Sow the seed on the top of a pot of soil mix and cover with a thin layer of sieved soil mix and then a topping of fine gravel. Water carefully and keep the soil moist. The pot can be left in a shaded, sheltered position outside, on the windowsill in a cool room or in a cool greenhouse. When the seed

Seeds can be collected from the attractive seed heads of ornamental onions.

Some bulbs such as this giant lily (*Cardiocrinum giganteum*) have large, flat seeds.

germinates most bulbs produce thin, grass-like leaves. Leave the seedlings in their pot to allow them to grow a small bulb before disturbing them. This may take a year or two. Then, when the seedlings are dormant, tip them out and pot the little bulbs up into a larger pot. A couple of years after that, they should be big enough to plant in the garden.

Some seed can be sown direct in the garden, where you want it to grow. *Tulipa sprengeri* and *Cyclamen coum* are good examples of plants that are easy to establish this way. You will find some bulbs do this anyway, naturally spreading themselves through a border.

Hardiness zones

Each bulb entry has a hardiness zone rating, as classified by the Royal Horticultural Society (RHS), which indicates the range of temperatures (from hot to freezing) that each particular plant tolerates. Plants in zones 1–2 require frost-free conditions year-round. Plants that can survive a frost are in zones 3 and above, with higher zone numbers indicating a lower temperature below freezing that the plant will tolerate. For further details of the individual hardiness ratings see the RHS website (https://www.rhs.org.uk/plants/trials-awards/award-of-garden-merit/rhs-hardiness-rating).

Plants

—

Autumn snowflake

Acis autumnalis, aka *Leucojum autumnale*

The delicate, white bells of the autumn snowflake are held on thin stems only a few centimetres above the ground. Waving in the breeze, a good clump of these flowers brings a magical touch to the autumn garden.

—

WHERE TO GROW
Grow in a raised bed, a rock garden or at the front of a sunny border, where the autumn snowflake will not be swamped by other plants. It needs good light soil that is well-drained, while retaining a little moisture.

HOW TO GROW
Plant the small bulbs in late summer and they will soon flower. The narrow, grass-like leaves last until spring.

GROWING TIP
Autumn snowflake is easily hidden by other plants so you could grow it in a pot that you put out on display when it is in flower.

Family Amaryllidaceae

Height
10–15cm/4–6in

Flowering time
Autumn

Hardiness
Zone 5

Position
Sunny and well-drained

CLOSELY RELATED
Acis is very similar to *Leucojum*, the larger spring snowflake, but DNA studies have shown they are separate genera.

African lily

Agapanthus aka Lily of the Nile, blue lily

Impressive, rounded umbels, in shades of blue, purple, white or sometimes pink, appear from the middle of summer, held high above strap-like leaves. Originating from southern Africa, these showy plants look great in an exotic or Mediterranean garden.

—

WHERE TO GROW

Grow in a warm, sheltered spot, against a wall or on a sunny slope. It needs protection from hard frost, but some are tougher than others.

HOW TO GROW

Plant in free-draining soil in spring, and water regularly during summer. In gardens where frosts are often below −5°C/23°F, grow in a pot that can be brought inside for the winter, although evergreen forms still need sunlight.

GROWING TIP

Deciduous forms such as *A. campanulatus* are the hardiest, dying down to fleshy rhizomes for the winter. A deep, dry mulch will protect the rhizomes from frost in a garden border.

Family	Amaryllidaceae
Height	45–150cm/18–60in
Flowering time	Mid- to late summer
Hardiness	Zones 3–4
Position	Hot and sunny

Agapanthus africanus

NOT ALL IN A NAME
Although known as African lily, *Agapanthus* is more closely related to the genus *Allium*, the onions (see page 30).

Ornamental onion

Allium

The dramatic, rounded heads of ornamental onions, in purple, pink or white, float above surrounding plants from late spring, adding a surreal flourish to a border. There are many varieties – some flowering later in the summer. Many varieties look good as cut flowers (see Making a cut-flower patch, page 94) and their seed heads are also attractive.

WHERE TO GROW

Plant in any sunny herbaceous border, in a gravel garden or among ornamental grasses, as long as the soil is never waterlogged (see Planting ornamental onions in a herbaceous border, page 34). Smaller varieties do well in pots.

HOW TO GROW

Most ornamental onion bulbs are best planted in autumn but can be left until early winter. Large bulbs need a deep hole. Plant among summer perennials that will grow to fill the gap once the ornamental onions have finished.

GROWING TIP

When planting the bulbs, scatter them among other plants, instead of clustering together in a group. This way, the flowers will lead your eye through the border.

Family Amaryllidaceae	
Height 15–150cm/6–60in	
Flowering time Late spring to late summer	
Hardiness Zone 6	
Position Full sun	

Allium senescens

GOOD ENOUGH TO EAT
Onions, leeks, chives, garlic and shallots are all varieties of *Allium*, as well as the ornamental garden bulbs.

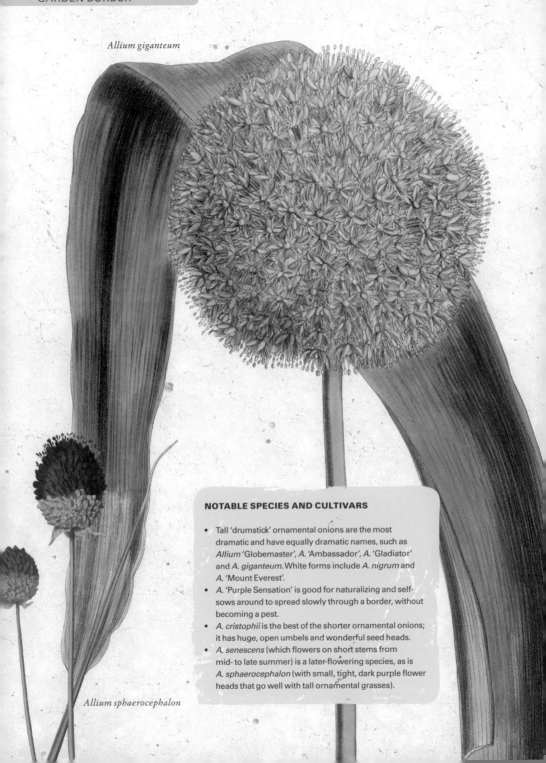

Allium giganteum

Allium sphaerocephalon

NOTABLE SPECIES AND CULTIVARS

- Tall 'drumstick' ornamental onions are the most
  dramatic and have equally dramatic names, such as
  Allium 'Globemaster', *A.* 'Ambassador', *A.* 'Gladiator'
  and *A. giganteum*. White forms include *A. nigrum* and
  A. 'Mount Everest'.
- *A.* 'Purple Sensation' is good for naturalizing and self-
  sows around to spread slowly through a border, without
  becoming a pest.
- *A. cristophii* is the best of the shorter ornamental onions;
  it has huge, open umbels and wonderful seed heads.
- *A. senescens* (which flowers on short stems from
  mid- to late summer) is a later-flowering species, as is
  A. sphaerocephalon (with small, tight, dark purple flower
  heads that go well with tall ornamental grasses).

Sicilian honey garlic

Allium siculum aka *Nectaroscordum siculum*,
Sicilian honey lily, Mediterranean bells

Sicilian honey garlic is now included in *Allium*, but bulbs
are still mostly sold as *Nectaroscordum*. The bell-shaped
flowers hang down as they open, held in a loose umbel
at the top of the tall stem; each one is pink with a green
base. As the seed pods develop, the flowers point back
upwards again.

Family	Amaryllidaceae
Height	75–120cm/30–40in
Flowering time	Spring
Hardiness	Zone 5
Position	Sunny and well-drained

WHERE TO GROW

This is an easy bulb for a sunny border or gravel garden,
where Sicilian honey garlic will rise above surrounding
plants, providing a strong vertical accent. The stems
persist well into summer as the seed heads develop.

HOW TO GROW

Plant bulbs in autumn. A position in full sun is best
but Sicilian honey garlic can tolerate some dappled
shade if the soil is not too wet in summer.

GROWING TIP

In a warm, sunny garden, Sicilian honey garlic can seed
around prolifically. To avoid it spreading too much, you
might need to remove the faded flower heads before
they scatter their seeds.

HOLLOW LEAVES
The leaves of Sicilian honey
garlic are triangular in cross
section and hollow. They
smell strongly of garlic.

Belladonna lily

Amaryllis belladonna aka Jersey lily

Sugar-pink trumpets appear in early autumn, before the leaves. Several blooms of this South African species can open at the top of the tall, upright stem and, when sheltered from the wind, a group of belladonna lilies can create a beautiful display.

—

Family Amaryllidaceae

Height
50–70cm/20–28in

Flowering time
Early autumn

Hardiness
Zone 4

Position
Sunny and sheltered

WHERE TO GROW

These bulbs thrive in the warmth and shelter at the base of a wall, facing the sun. In gardens where frosts are rare, plant near the front of a border for a colour boost at the end of summer.

HOW TO GROW

Position the top of the large bulb at the soil surface; there is no need to bury it deep underground. Light, free-draining soil is best as belladonna lilies like to be kept dry when they are dormant.

GROWING TIP

Add some gravel to the soil, beneath the bulbs, to improve drainage and help keep the base of the bulb dry in summer.

BIGENERIC HYBRID
Belladonna lily has been crossed with another autumn-flowering bulb, nerine, to create × *Amarine*, which is shorter than *Amaryllis* and has more trumpet-shaped flowers than nerine.

Planting ornamental onions in a herbaceous border

After the flourish of spring bulbs begins to wane, ornamental onions (*Allium*) take over, signalling the beginning of summer. When they flower, summer perennials are already growing upwards. It is the tall drumstick ornamental onions that can rise above this new growth and display their pompom-like flower heads above the greenery.

The time to plant ornamental onion bulbs is autumn, but you will have to clear some space among the herbaceous perennials. It is very effective to scatter these bulbs through a border, front to back, so when they flower they give depth to the planting. Take some time to place the bulbs on the ground to achieve the effect you want, remembering that some, such as A. 'Ambassador', can reach well above 1m/3ft tall. Once you are happy with their placement, dig a hole for each bulb. The bulbs can be quite large so you need a deep hole. Use a trowel or bulb planter for this job. Push the bulb planter into the ground as far as it will go; when you lift it out it will bring a plug of soil with it. Place the bulb in the hole. Then use the planter to make another hole and the first plug of soil will be pushed out the top and can be put in the first hole to cover the bulb.

Ornamental onion bulbs begin to grow in winter, and throughout spring the leaves will get longer. Some larger ornamental onions make quite impressive clumps of foliage. When they flower, the leaves are already dying back, but by then the herbaceous perennials should be growing up to hide them. When the ornamental onions have finished, the perennials move in to fill the space. It is the perfect arrangement.

1   The tall drumstick ornamental onions have large bulbs that need deep holes when planted.
2   In autumn, clear space between the herbaceous plants, then scatter ornamental onion bulbs on the ground. They are then ready to plant.
3   Use a bulb planter or trowel to make the hole. Here the soil from the previous hole is being pushed out as the planter is pushed down.
4   *Allium* 'Ambassador' is one of the tallest ornamental onions and makes a great display in early summer.
5   *Allium hollandicum* 'Purple Sensation' is smaller than some ornamental onions but it seeds around to gradually colonize a border.

Windflower

Anemone

There are many different species of *Anemone* but it is the
Mediterranean windflowers with their small, knobbly tubers
that can be planted like bulbs. *Anemone blanda* can carpet the
ground with blue or white, daisy-like flowers and *A. coronaria*
has richly coloured, bowl-shaped blooms.

—

WHERE TO GROW

Anemone blanda does well in sun or dappled shade and
can be grown in a woodland garden (see Planting a carpet
of windflowers, page 50). *A. coronaria* prefers a hot, sunny
position, on a grassy bank or in a gravel garden.

HOW TO GROW

Plant the little tubers in autumn, scattered through a border.
They will slowly spread by themselves. *Anemone blanda* can
be used as underplanting for taller spring bulbs; *A.b.* 'White
Splendour' is a popular form.

GROWING TIP

Soak the tubers in lukewarm water for a few hours before
planting, to get them soaking up water and prompt them
into growth.

Family Ranunculaceae	
Height 10–30cm/4–12in	
Flowering time Early to mid-spring	
Hardiness Zone 5	
Position Partial shade or full sun	

Anemone blanda

STUFF OF LEGENDS
The name Anemone is
probably a corruption of
Naaman, whose scattered
blood produced the blood-red
A. coronaria, according to
Greek legend.

Cobra lily

Arisaema aka Jack-in-the-pulpit

The weirdest flowers of any bulb belong to the cobra lilies. Spooky, hooded spathes, often with striking markings, are held on stiff, straight stems. A cluster of these resembles a group of meerkats peering out of their burrow.

—

WHERE TO GROW

Humus-rich soil and dappled shade are best so plant in a woodland garden or partially shaded border. Avoid soil that dries out in summer, which is the main growing season for cobra lilies.

HOW TO GROW

Plant the tubers in late autumn. Once you see the shoots appear in spring, make sure the soil does not dry out until the leaves die back in late summer.

GROWING TIP

You can also grow cobra lilies in large pots. Many have attractive leaves as well as the strange inflorescences, and they make a striking feature in a shady corner of the garden.

Family Araceae	
Height 30–100cm/12–40in	
Flowering time Late spring to early summer	
Hardiness Zone 4	
Position Cool and partial shade	

IN THE HOOD
The flowers of cobra lilies are tiny, clustered together and hidden at the base of the central spadix. It is the hooded spathe that is often attractively patterned.

Arisaema ringens

Italian arum

Arum italicum aka Italian lords and ladies

Italian arum has attractively veined and mottled, arrow-shaped leaves, especially in *A. italicum* subsp. *italicum* 'Marmoratum'. The leaves grow through the winter, and in spring the wide, pale green spathes appear, followed by bright orange but poisonous berries.

—

WHERE TO GROW

Being suitable for sun or dappled shade, Italian arum can be grown in a variety of situations, as long as the soil is not wet all the time. Use it as winter ground cover in herbaceous borders or under deciduous trees.

HOW TO GROW

A few tubers planted in autumn will make a nice patch of foliage that will slowly spread, as they increase by making offsets from the main plant. Italian arum is best avoided if you have young children who may eat the berries.

GROWING TIP

Italian arum dies down for the summer so plant the tubers deep enough that summer flowers can be planted in the same spot – 15cm (6in) deep should be fine.

Family Araceae

Height
15–30cm/6–12in

Flowering time
Spring

Hardiness
Zone 6

Position
Full sun or dappled shade

COMMON OR GARDEN?
A similar species, *Arum maculatum*, has more than 100 common names including cuckoo pint, parson-in-the-pulpit and lords and ladies.

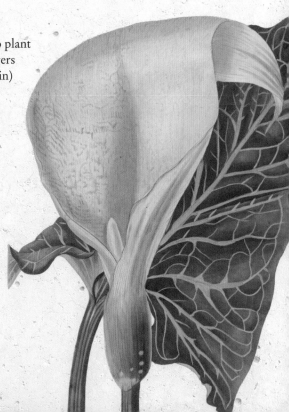

Bellevalia

Bellevalia

These small bulbs are similar to the grape hyacinths (*Muscari*), with little flowers clustered on top of a straight stem. Many are in shades of cream or brownish yellow, but it is the dark purple or intense blue species such as *Bellevalia pycnantha* that are most attractive.

—

WHERE TO GROW

Bellevalias do well under deciduous trees and shrubs in a mixed border, where they get plenty of light and moisture in their growing season or try them in raised bed where you will get to see their flowers up close.

HOW TO GROW

These bulbs are easy to grow in soil that dries out a little in summer. Plant them in autumn in a sunny border or try some in a pot but keep them moist in winter and spring.

GROWING TIP

Individually, these plants are quite insignificant so plant the bulbs in clusters or drifts that will make a greater impact in a border.

Family Asparagaceae	
Height 15–20cm/6–8in	
Flowering time Spring	
Hardiness Zone 5	
Position Full sun or dappled shade	

BOTANICAL PEDIGREE
Bellevalia is named after French botanist Pierre Richer de Belleval, who founded Montpelier Botanic Garden in the sixteenth century.

Bellevalia paradoxa

Cluster lily

Brodiaea

These rarely grown corms are worth trying in the garden for their star-like, purple flowers in early summer. The one you are most likely to find for sale is *B. californica*, which has stiff, upright stems holding a loose umbel of up to fifteen flowers.

—

WHERE TO GROW

Brodiaeas are plants for a rock garden, raised bed or sloping border to ensure they do not sit in damp soil in summer. They also need a sheltered position and plenty of sun.

HOW TO GROW

Gritty, well-drained soil is needed for these corms to do well but in the right spot they add a colourful highlight after most spring bulbs are finished.

GROWING TIP

The leaves of cluster lily grow all winter so can look tatty by the time the bulbs flower. Therefore, plant them among low-growing plants such as sun roses (*Helianthemum*), which will hide the cluster lily foliage.

Family Asparagaceae	
Height 10–30cm/4–12in	
Flowering time Early summer	
Hardiness Zone 3	
Position Full sun and well-drained	

WILD WEST
Cluster lilies come from the summer-dry hills and mountains of western North America and *B. californica* is found wild only in California.

Brodiaea coronaria

Mariposa lily

Calochortus aka fairy lantern, globe lily, star tulip

The flowers with beautifully coloured petals held on delicate, wiry stems, with narrow leaves, make mariposa lilies among the most attractive spring bulbs. They are not the easiest to grow but worth the effort if you have the patience to try.

Family Liliaceae	
Height 10–30cm/4–12in	
Flowering time Spring	
Hardiness Zone 3	
Position Dry, sunny and sheltered	

WHERE TO GROW

These exquisite bulbs need warmth and sunshine to thrive. Plant in a sunny, sheltered spot or, even better, a pot that you can protect from the cold and rain.

HOW TO GROW

Sandy, free-draining soil is important, and not too much rain. This normally means growing mariposa lilies in a pot, in an unheated greenhouse or cold frame, unless you garden in a Mediterranean climate.

GROWING TIP

The key to success when watering is to keep bulbs mostly dry until growth appears in early spring. Once mariposa lilies have died down, give them no water at all over summer and autumn.

BUTTERFLY FLOWER
Mariposa is Spanish for 'butterfly', an apt name for these beautifully coloured and patterned blooms.

Calochortus elegans

41

Planting tender bulbs in a pot

Not all bulbs are hardy enough to grow in a garden. Some need protection from freezing weather but they can be put outside for summer, either in pots or planted out, once there is little risk of frost. Such half-hardy plants include bugle lily (*Watsonia*), Cape cowslip (*Lachenalia*) and florist's cyclamen (*Cyclamen persicum*).

Bulbs that need extra warmth year-round are classed as tender. This extra warmth is especially important if they are winter growers. If you want to cultivate them, you should keep them indoors, like a house plant. All you need is a light windowsill, an attractive pot, some soil and the bulb itself.

Amaryllis (*Hippeastrum*) are among the most dramatic and popular of the tender bulbs. They can be bought in autumn or early winter, ready for planting. The large bulbs often have roots showing as well. These roots and the lower part of the bulb should be in the soil mix (see Growing bulbs in pots, page 20) but the top half or more can be left out in the open. The pot needs to be only a little wider than the bulb, leaving at most 2.5cm/1in between the pot's rim and the bulb. Water the soil, position the pot in the warm and wait for the shoot to develop.

Once growth starts, you can move the pot to a cooler position in the light, near a window. Keep turning the pot so the shoots do not bend towards the light. You will soon have a display of those amazing trumpet blooms. After flowering, cut off the stem but let the leaves continue to grow, making food for the bulb to flower another year.

1. The bulbs of amaryllis are large and often have roots growing out of the base when you buy them.
2. Plant each bulb so its roots and base are covered in soil mix, but the rest of the bulb is exposed. Keep the soil moist.
3. Once the shoot begins to develop, make sure the bulb is in good light. The shoot will grow towards the light so you should keep turning the pot to keep it straight.
4. Eventually, the fat buds will open to reveal huge, trumpet-like blooms. The open flowers can make the plant top-heavy so use some wire supports to help keep it upright.

Camas

Camassia aka quamash, Indian hyacinth

These large bulbs produce strap-like basal leaves and a tall spike of many pale to dark blue flowers. Like overgrown bluebells but with flowers all round the stem, camas make the greatest impact when planted in drifts.

—

WHERE TO GROW
Camas need plenty of sunlight and moisture in winter and spring, so grow them among spring and summer perennials in a sunny border or in grass under deciduous trees.

HOW TO GROW
In autumn, plant the bulbs in soil that drains well but retains some moisture year-round. If grown in grass, remember to leave mowing the grass until the camas leaves have died back completely.

GROWING TIP
In the wild, camas are often found in seasonally boggy ground so make sure your bulbs do not dry out, especially when in growth.

Family Asparagaceae	
Height 50–100cm/20–40in	
Flowering time Late spring	
Hardiness Zone 4	
Position Sun or dappled shade	

Camassia quamash

SUSTENANCE
The bulbs of camas can be eaten and were a food source for native Americans long before they became garden plants.

Giant lily

Cardiocrinum giganteum aka giant Himalayan lily

A giant among bulbs, this plant produces several huge, white, trumpet-shaped flowers on tall, leafy stems that can reach over 2m/7ft. The bulbs are massive and can take several years to flower, but they are worth the wait.

—

WHERE TO GROW
Such big, leafy plants need plenty of moisture. They come from the slopes of the Himalaya that have high summer rainfall so plant giant lilies in a cool woodland or partially shaded border.

HOW TO GROW
Plant the bulbs in humus-rich, moist but not waterlogged soil. Even large bulbs may take a year or two to flower. Give them plenty of water when growing.

GROWING TIP
After putting all its energy into producing the impressive flowering shoot, the bulb dies but it will make offsets that can be removed and grown on to flowering size.

Family Liliaceae

Height
1–2.5m/3–8ft

Flowering time
Summer

Hardiness
Zone 5

Position
Cool summer shade

WAIT FOR IT
Enormous flowers are followed by huge seed pods containing paper-like seeds. From seed to flowering can take seven years or more.

45

Meadow saffron

Colchicum aka naked ladies, autumn crocus

Appearing as summer fades into autumn, the goblet-shaped flowers of meadow saffron are usually a shade of violet, magenta or pink. They emerge from the ground before their leaves, hence the common name of naked ladies.

—

WHERE TO GROW

Whether planted in dappled shade on the edge of a woodland garden, at the base of a tree in a raised bed or in a lawn, meadow saffron is an adaptable plant that needs free-draining soil.

HOW TO GROW

The corms of meadow saffron are sold at the end of summer so buy and plant them as soon as you can and they will flower in a few weeks or less.

GROWING TIP

Be careful what you plant meadow saffron with, as the leaves can be huge compared to its flowers and will last through to late spring. They can smother delicate spring flowers such as primroses (*Primula vulgaris*) and wood anemones (*Anemone nemorosa*).

Family	Colchicaceae
Height	7–15cm/3–6in
Flowering time	Autumn
Hardiness	Zone 5
Position	Full sun or partial shade

NOTABLE SPECIES AND CULTIVARS

- *C. autumnale* is the true meadow saffron, a plant of meadows in Western Europe, and it does well in the garden.
- *C. speciosum* has larger flowers and there are a number of varieties, such as deep pink *C.s.* 'Atrorubens' and white *C.s.* 'Album'.
- *C.* 'Rosy Dawn' has violet-pink flowers with white centres.
- *C.* 'Waterily' is an unusual form with double flowers made up of a cluster of narrow petals; more novelty than beauty.
- *C. agrippinum* and *C. cilicicum* are among several species of *Colchicum* that have attractive, tessellated patterns on their petals.
- The most common colour of meadow saffron is pink, and the usual flowering time is autumn, but there are spring-flowering species such as *C. luteum*, which has yellow blooms that appear with the leaves.

Colchicum speciosum

ANCIENT REMEDY
The autumn crocus is poisonous and the origin of the drug colchicine, used to treat a number of illnesses. It was first recorded as a treatment for gout in the first century AD.

Lily of the valley

Convallaria majalis aka May bells, May lily

Lily of the valley has dainty, white bells hanging from a delicate, gently arching stem above wide leaves. It is the sweet scent that has made this many people's favourite spring flower, as well as the fact that it is so easy to grow.

WHERE TO GROW

This is a traditional cottage-garden flower that does well in a variety of situations, as long as it is not too dry or too wet. It should thrive in partial shade, under deciduous trees or shrubs.

HOW TO GROW

Lily of the valley grows from thin rhizomes and is usually sold in pots in spring, when the leaves are already showing. This is a good time to buy and plant them in your garden.

GROWING TIP

Plants gradually spread to make dense clumps that can be divided in late spring. If plants are failing to flower, it is often because the clump needs splitting up and given more room.

Family	Convallariaceae
Height	10–15cm/4–6in
Flowering time	Late spring
Hardiness	Zone 7
Position	Sun or partial shade

MAYFLOWER
In France and Germany, lily of the valley is a symbol of May Day and called *muguet de mai* or *Maiblume.*

Spring fumewort

Corydalis solida aka spring corydalis, bird-in-a-bush

Growing from small, rounded, pebble-like tubers, the spring fumewort has delicate, fern-like, blue-green leaves that keep low to the ground and show off its short spikes of pinkish to red, tubular flowers in spring.

—

WHERE TO GROW

Spring fumewort needs plenty of light in spring, but does not want too much heat in summer, so a site under deciduous trees is ideal, or plant in a partially shaded raised bed or rock garden.

HOW TO GROW

Plant spring fumewort tubers in autumn, in well-drained but moisture-retentive soil. Scatter through a woodland garden border. Over time, self-sown seedlings will fill the gaps.

GROWING TIP

This is a low-growing plant that looks best when mixed with other small, ephemeral spring flowers such as anemones and blue squills (*Scilla*).

Family Papaveraceae

Height
5–10cm/2–4in

Flowering time
Spring

Hardiness
Zone 5

Position
Partial shade

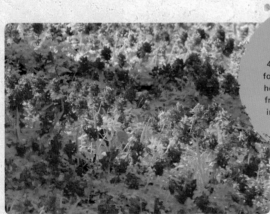

CHINA BLUE
There are more than 400 species of *Corydalis* found across the northern hemisphere, but most are from China, including the intriguing blue-flowered *C. flexuosa*.

49

Planting a carpet of windflowers

One of the many wonderful sights of spring is a woodland floor covered with the flowers of anemones. You can recreate this scene using Grecian windflower (*Anemone blanda*) – and you do not need a woodland to grow them. They only grow a few centimetres tall so are perfect for carpeting the ground, along with other early bulbs.

Grecian windflowers grow from small, black or dark brown, knobbly tubers that are sold alongside spring-flowering bulbs. The tubers are hard and dry when you buy them so soak them in lukewarm water for a few hours before planting, to get them absorbing moisture. Grecian windflowers can be planted under deciduous trees, under shrubs or in a border of summer perennials. Then once you have chosen a place to grow them, clear away the soil to a depth of about 5cm/2in and place the tubers on the ground. Cover them with the soil and lightly firm. Give them some water to start them off but then leave the rain to keep the soil moist. They start growing in winter and flower in early spring. The flowers look like large daisies, in shades of blue, violet and white. One of the most popular varieties is *A.b.* 'White Splendour'.

Although you may start with only a small patch, under a shrub or at the front of a border, the windflowers will slowly spread and one day you will have that carpet of blooms.

1 The dry tubers of Grecian windflower are hard and knobbly. Soak in water for a few hours before planting.
2 Clear a patch of ground and dig out some soil to make a wide hole about 5cm/2in deep.
3 Place the tubers evenly over the bottom of the hole.
4 Push the soil back over the tubers and lightly firm before giving them a water.
5 In spring, the Grecian windflowers will flower, and over time they will gradually spread by themselves.

PLANTING A CARPET OF WINDFLOWERS   51

Swamp lily

Crinum × powellii aka Powell's lily

Widely strap-shaped leaves surround lily-like trumpets, giving this bulb an exotic appearance well suited to a subtropical garden. The pink or white flowers emerge on a leafless stem from the top of the large bulb during late summer.

—

WHERE TO GROW

Plant the bulbs in fertile, humus-rich soil in a light, sheltered position, such as along a sunny wall or in a courtyard garden. They can be grown in a conservatory or greenhouse in regions where frosts are common.

HOW TO GROW

Plant swamp lily bulbs so the tops are poking above soil level. The leaves can be semi-evergreen, lasting year-round in frost-free gardens, but the main growing season is summer, when plants should be given plenty of water.

GROWING TIP

If frosts are common, grow swamp lilies in a large pot that you keep frost-free during winter. Repot every spring to provide fresh soil, as they can be hungry plants.

Family Amaryllidaceae

Height
50–150cm/20–60in

Flowering time
Late summer

Hardiness
Zone 4

Position
Sunny and sheltered

HYBRID VIGOUR
There are more than 100 species of *Crinum*, most of them tender, but *C. × powellii* is a garden hybrid that is vigorous and relatively hardy.

Montbretia

Crocosmia

Along with their fresh green, sword-like leaves, montbretias have bright summer flowers in shades of red, orange and yellow. There are many different named cultivars – some flowering in early summer, others later.

WHERE TO GROW

These southern African plants need plenty of light, so a sunny border is essential. Grow alongside summer perennials or mingle with ornamental grasses such as hair grass (*Deschampsia*) and purple moor grass (*Molinia*).

HOW TO GROW

Plant the dry corms in autumn in soil that is not too wet over winter. Montbretias put up their leaves in spring. Growing plants can be bought in pots in early summer, to plant straight out in the garden.

GROWING TIP

The corms are relatively cheap so buy plenty as there can be a high failure rate, especially in cold, damp soil. The more expensive containerized plants are sometimes easier to establish in a garden.

Family Iridaceae
Height 30–100cm/12–40in
Flowering time Summer
Hardiness Zone 4
Position Full sun

Crocosmia × crocosmiiflora

SPACE INVADER
The common montbretia *C. × crocosmiiflora* can be invasive, especially in coastal regions where frosts are rare, but most garden forms are better behaved.

Crocus

Crocus

Crocuses are the familiar heralds of spring that are grown in many gardens and come in a rainbow of colours. The goblet-shaped flowers emerge close to the ground, usually signalling the end of winter, but there are some equally beautiful autumn species of crocus.

WHERE TO GROW

Any sunny position is fine for crocuses, but they look best in a lawn or scattered through a border, at the base of a wall or in pots on a patio, alongside other early spring bulbs. See also Making a bulb lasagne, page 58.

HOW TO GROW

Any free-draining soil is suitable for crocuses. Plant the corms of autumn species in late summer and they will soon flower, before their leaves appear. Spring species can be planted anytime in autumn.

GROWING TIP

In a lawn, peel back the turf; plant the corms and replace the turf carefully; they will easily push through the grass.

Family Iridaceae
Height   8–12cm/3–5in
Flowering time   Spring or autumn
Hardiness   Zone 6
Position   Sunny and open

SELF-LEVELLING
Crocuses like to be planted relatively deep, usually more than three times the size of the corm. If not planted that deep, they have contractile roots that will pull the corm down to the right depth.

Crocus speciosus

Crocus chrysanthus

NOTABLE SPECIES AND CULTIVARS

- *C. tommasinianus*, sometimes called little Tommies, is the earliest spring-flowering species. Once established, it will cover a border with bright purple blooms, opening wide in the early spring sunshine.
- Closely following are the various named forms of *C. chrysanthus* and *C. biflorus*, such as *C.b.* 'Blue Pearl' and *C. c.* 'Cream Beauty'. Later in spring come the richly coloured goblets of the Dutch hybrids, the largest and most robust crocuses.
- *C. speciosus* is the most commonly grown autumh species. The flowers are pale purple, with intricate veining and there is a pure white form, *C.s.* 'Albus'.
- *C. nudiflorus* and *C. goulimyi* are excellent but less common autumn species.
- *C. sativus* has deep orange styles at the centres of purple blooms. The styles are picked for the costly spice saffron, once cultivated throughout the Mediterranean region and western Asia, as well as the UK, giving its name to the market town of Saffron Walden.

Cyclamen

Cyclamen aka sow bread

The intricately patterned leaves of cyclamen can cover the ground and are reason enough to grow these plants. The pink, magenta or white flowers, with swept-back petals, are held on short, arching stems above the leaves.

—

WHERE TO GROW

Cyclamen can be grown in a variety of locations, including at the front of a border, in a lawn or in a raised bed. They need good drainage, so try them under deciduous trees and shrubs in a mixed border.

HOW TO GROW

Plant the rounded tubers near the surface; do not bury too deeply. The dormant tubers do not like to dry out too much so it is usually more successful to establish cyclamen from growing plants that are sold in flower.

GROWING TIP

The seeds are held in big, rounded pods and are loved by ants. Allow the ants to distribute the seeds around your garden, and in a few years you may have hundreds of cyclamen popping up.

Family Primulaceae	
Height 5–20cm/2–8in	
Flowering time All seasons	
Hardiness Zones 3–5	
Position Sun or partial shade	

Cyclamen hederifolium

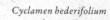

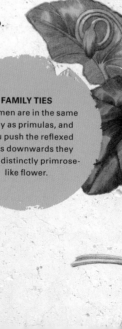

FAMILY TIES
Cyclamen are in the same family as primulas, and if you push the reflexed petals downwards they form a distinctly primrose-like flower.

Cyclamen coum

NOTABLE SPECIES

There is a cyclamen to flower in every season and possibly every month of the year.

- *C. hederifolium* (ivy-leaved cyclamen) is the most commonly grown species. It can flower from late summer, and the attractive leaves last all winter.
- *C. coum* is the best winter-flowering species. Appearing in the coldest, darkest months, this diminutive species makes a good companion to snowdrops (*Galanthus*).
- *C. repandum* (a good woodland plant) and the tender *C. persicum* (which has been used to breed the popular florist's cyclamen) are popular spring-flowering species.
- *C. purpurascens*, sometimes sold as *C. europaeum*, provides summer flowers. Mainly grown by enthusiasts, it has too much competition from other summer flowers to make an impact in the garden.

Cyclamen repandum

Making a bulb lasagne

It may seem strange to link a pot of bulbs with an Italian dish, but just like lasagne this project involves making layers – not with pasta but with bulbs. The idea is that the different bulbs either flower together, making a fantastic spring display, or they flower in succession, one starting to bloom while another is fading.

You need a large pot or half-barrel, some soil mix (see Growing bulbs in pots, page 20) and a selection of bulbs. A good selection would be crocuses to flower first, followed by some of the smaller daffodils such as *Narcissus bulbocodium*, and tulips.

Fill the pot to about two-thirds full with a free-draining, loam-based soil mix. Large bulbs should be planted deep so they should go in first. Thus, place the tulips as the base layer of bulbs, towards the centre of the pot. Cover these with soil mix and plant the next layer, the daffodils, over the top but avoid placing a bulb directly above a tulip bulb on the base layer. The top layer is the crocus corms, placed towards the rim of the pot so their flowers are not hidden by the leaves of the other bulbs.

Fill the pot to its rim with the rest of the soil mix and water well. Let the soil dry out a little before watering again. Once leaves appear, you can water more frequently. By spring you should have a wonderful display of flowers that will last a few weeks.

Other bulbs to try planting in this way are grape hyacinths (*Muscari*), the smaller fritillaries, squills such as *Scilla siberica*, hyacinths, spring starflowers (*Ipheion uniflorum*) or reticulate irises.

1 Choose a selection of bulbs that will look good together or that will flower at slightly different times: here tulip (top), crocus (right) and daffodil (left).
2 Plant the tulips first, about a third of the way down the pot.
3 This shows the three layers of bulbs. Tulips at the bottom, then daffodils and finally the crocuses on the top layer. See how the bulbs are placed to avoid planting one directly over another.
4 Once all the bulbs and corms are planted, cover them will more soil mix to just below the rim, then water well.
5 In spring you will have a wonderful pot of bulbs flowering in succession. Here the crocuses have finished, but the daffodils and tulips are still going strong.

Firecracker flower

Dichelostemma ida-maia

This unusual corm from California and Oregon has a tall stem that holds a dense umbel of pendent, narrowly tubular, crimson-red flowers with pale green tips. In the wild, the flowers are pollinated by hummingbirds.

—

WHERE TO GROW

Plant in a city, courtyard or sheltered coastal garden. In regions where frosts are rare, try in a gravel garden, raised bed or rock garden.

HOW TO GROW

Plant the small corms in autumn, in free-draining soil. The flower stems will push through emerging summer perennials, ornamental grasses or low shrubs such as sun roses (*Helianthemum*).

GROWING TIP

The tall stems can be flattened by the wind so grow firecracker flowers among other plants that will provide some support in spring.

Family Asparagaceae

Height
50–100cm/20–40in

Flowering time
Spring

Hardiness
Zone 4

Position
Sunny and sheltered

LOCAL KNOWLEDGE
This plant is said to commemorate Ida May, daughter of a stagecoach driver who pointed out this plant to an early botanist studying in California.

Angel's fishing rod

Dierama aka wandflower, hairbell

Thin, wiry stems arch out high from a clump of narrowly linear, iris-like leaves. Pretty, bell-shaped flowers in shades of pink, purple, violet or red are strung out along the stem, hanging down delicately and fluttering in the breeze.

—

WHERE TO GROW

Grow angel's fishing rod in a gravel garden or border. It needs warmth and moisture in summer, but the corms do not want to be in wet soil over the winter.

HOW TO GROW

Corms can be planted in spring, but as most species are semi-evergreen it is more likely you will buy them in pots, ready to plant in your garden. Plants resent disturbance and may not flower for a couple of years after moving.

GROWING TIP

Angel's fishing rod can make fairly dense clumps, but it does not do so well if overcrowded by other plants. Give it plenty of room so it can make the most of the sunshine.

Family Iridaceae	
Height 60–150cm/24–60in	
Flowering time Summer	
Hardiness Zone 4	
Position Sunny and sheltered	

Dierama pulcherrimum

AFRICAN BEGINNINGS
Most angel's fishing rods come from summer-rainfall regions of southern Africa – a rich source of summer-flowering bulbs for the garden.

Dragon arum

Dracunculus vulgaris aka dragon's tongue, dragon lily

Dragon arum is a tall plant with a mottled stem, wide leaves and a striking, purple spathe surrounding a dark purple to black central spadix. It is not a thing of beauty but it is fascinating and bizarre – certainly a talking point in the garden.

—

WHERE TO GROW

This tuberous perennial does well under deciduous trees in gardens where frosts below –5°C/23°F are rare. Plant in a border or a woodland clearing, in humus-rich but not waterlogged soil.

HOW TO GROW

The large tubers need planting deep, usually about 15cm/6in down, in autumn or early spring. In the right place they need little attention, but the flowers have an unpleasant smell so do not grow dragon arum by a window.

GROWING TIP

When dragon arum blooms, the huge inflorescence can weigh down the stem, so stake it with a strong stick or bamboo cane, to keep the plant upright.

Family Araceae	
Height 100–150cm/40–60in	
Flowering time Late spring	
Hardiness Zone 4	
Position Sun or partial shade	

STINKER
The flowers of dragon arum are pollinated by flies, and the plant attracts them by emitting a foul stench from the spathe, like rotting meat.

Winter aconite

Eranthis hyemalis aka aconite

Winter aconite is an invaluable flower for the winter garden. Its little, rounded cups of bright yellow are held on short stems, just above the divided leaves. When sprinkled through a border, these diminutive flowers lift the spirits on a cold, grey day.

—

WHERE TO GROW
These tuberous perennials need to make the most of the light in the shortest days of the year, so plant them in an open border or under the bare branches of deciduous trees and shrubs. They do best in alkaline soil but will grow in most conditions.

HOW TO GROW
In autumn, plant the little, knobbly tubers in humus-rich but free-draining soil that does not dry out completely in summer. Scatter them in loose drifts, and they will seed around, gradually building up a small colony.

GROWING TIP
Winter aconite is an ideal companion to snowdrops (*Galanthus*), *Iris reticulata*, early crocuses and *Cyclamen coum*, all requiring similar conditions and creating a tapestry of winter bulbs.

Family Ranunculaceae

Height
5–10cm/2–4in

Flowering time
Winter

Hardiness
Zone 6

Position
Sun or partial shade

EASY OPTION
Eranthis is a genus of nine species, but *E. hyemalis* is by far the easiest to grow. It is found wild in Europe and naturalized in Britain.

Foxtail lily

Eremurus aka desert candle

Who can resist the tall, waving wands of foxtail lily, with its long, dense cluster of colourful flowers held high above surrounding plants on a leafless stem? But it needs the right conditions – otherwise your pleasure will be short-lived.
—

WHERE TO GROW
Foxtail lilies need plenty of sunshine and well-drained soil to survive. Plant in a dry garden or gravel garden and do not overcrowd with other plants. The narrowly linear leaves are at ground level and do not want to be shaded out.

HOW TO GROW
Long fleshy roots, radiating from a central growing point, look like a starfish. They can be brittle so handle carefully when planting in early spring, and leave the crown just below soil level.

GROWING TIP
To improve drainage around the roots, place the crown on a mound of gravel before covering with soil. Mark the spot with a cane until shoots show, so you do not damage them when planting close by.

Family	Asphodelaceae
Height	100–250cm/40–100in
Flowering time	Early summer
Hardiness	Zone 6
Position	Sunny and well-drained

Eremurus spectabilis

DESERT CANDLE
Foxtail lilies grow in dry, rocky, open landscapes in western and central Asia, where winter is very cold, and summer is long and dry.

Dog's-tooth violet

Erythronium aka trout lily, glacier lily

Some of the most elegant and graceful spring bulbs belong to the genus *Erythronium*. The pendent flowers have gently arching petals that sweep back as they open, above plain green to mottled or marbled foliage.

—

WHERE TO GROW

Dog's-tooth violets need open woodland conditions, where they flower before the tree leaves block out the sun. Plant in a cool, partially shaded border or under deciduous trees, with humus-rich but not waterlogged soil (see also Planting bulbs in a shady border, page 78).

HOW TO GROW

Plant bulbs in autumn, soon after buying, as they do not want to dry out at this time of year. They will take a while to establish but eventually make good-sized clumps that can then be divided to spread through a border.

GROWING TIP

The long, thin bulbs are best planted vertically, with the most pointed end upwards. The hole should be deep enough to fit the bulb and cover it with at least 10cm/4in soil.

Family	Liliaceae
Height	10–30cm/4–12in
Flowering time	Spring
Hardiness	Zone 5
Position	Cool and partial shade

MAKING A POINT
The common name of dog's-tooth violet comes from the shape of the bulb, which looks like a canine tooth.

Erythronium dens-canis

NOTABLE SPECIES AND CULTIVARS

- *E. dens-canis* (European dog's-tooth violet) is one of the smallest species, to only 10cm/4in tall, but has pretty, pink to violet flowers and attractively mottled leaves. It can be grown in thin grass under trees.
- Most species are from North America, including the creamy white *E. californicum* and beautiful, vigorous *E.c.* 'White Beauty'.
- *E. tuolumnense* is another Californian species, with golden yellow flowers and plain green leaves. Even better is a hybrid between this and *E. californicum* called *E.* 'Pagoda'. This is one of the easiest to grow and has four or more sulphur-yellow blooms on each stem. It can reach 30cm/12in tall.
- *E. hendersonii* has lilac-pink flowers and in *E. revolutum* they are shades of pink. Both are beautiful bulbs and will spread by seed.

Erythronium hendersonii

Pineapple lily

Eucomis aka pineapple flower

Exotic, leafy plants that range from small, compact varieties to huge, dramatic forms, but all have long racemes tightly packed with many small, pretty flowers and topped by a tuft of leafy bracts. Some, such as *E. comosa* 'Sparkling Burgundy', have attractive, purple foliage.

Family Asparagaceae

Height
30–150cm/12–60in

Flowering time
Summer

Hardiness
Zone 4

Position
Sunny and sheltered

WHERE TO GROW

Set in a sunny herbaceous border in gardens where frosts below –5°C/23°F are rare, in humus-rich but well-drained soil. Pineapple lilies also make excellent pot plants, especially the small forms, when brought outside for summer but protected from hard frosts in winter.

HOW TO GROW

Plant bulbs in early spring, and once growing make sure they do not dry out. Too much winter wet is more likely to kill pineapple lily than frost, but it needs protecting from frosts below –10°C/14°F.

GROWING TIP

When planting the bulbs, bear in mind how big the leaves may grow. Some of the largest forms need at least 30cm/12in between them and are best at the back of a border.

Eucomis bicolor

DO NOT FOLLOW YOUR NOSE
The flowers are scented, but they are pollinated by flies, so the unpleasant smell is attractive to flies, not humans.

Fritillary

Fritillaria

This genus comprises a diverse range of beautiful spring bulbs, from dainty snake's-head fritillary (*F. meleagris*) to the stately crown imperial (*F. imperialis*). Their bell-shaped flowers face downwards, and in some are intricately marked inside. There are several easy-to-grow species.

—

WHERE TO GROW

Most fritillaries for the garden are best grown in a partially shaded border, under deciduous trees or in a sunny border. Snake's-head fritillary can be grown in a damp lawn where the soil never dries out completely (see Creating a drift of snake's-head fritillary, page 70).

HOW TO GROW

Plant bulbs in autumn, in moisture-retentive but well-drained soil. Small species can easily be swamped by other plants, but the taller species such as crown imperials will rise above them.

GROWING TIP

The small species, except *F. meleagris*, are great plants for growing in a pot. This also makes it easier to look at them closely so you can appreciate the delicate patterns inside the flowers.

Family Liliaceae	
Height 10–150cm/4–60in	
Flowering time Spring	
Hardiness Zone 5	
Position Sun or dappled shade	

SWEET NECTAR
Look inside the flower and you will see a clearly marked nectary at the base of each petal, sometimes dripping with nectar.

Fritillaria meleagris

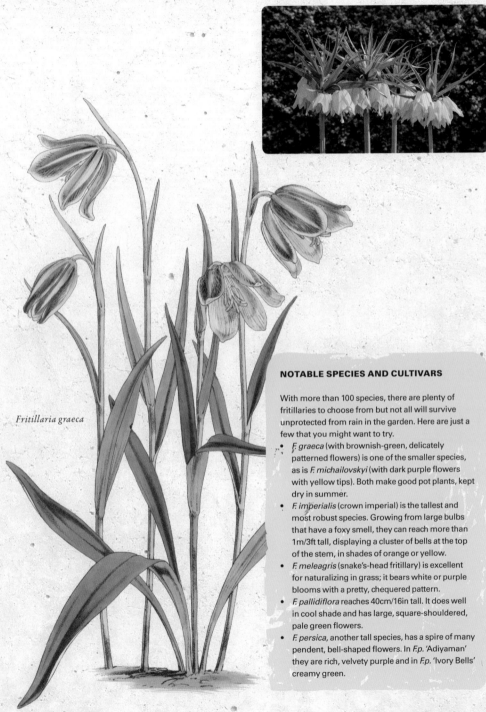

Fritillaria graeca

NOTABLE SPECIES AND CULTIVARS

With more than 100 species, there are plenty of fritillaries to choose from but not all will survive unprotected from rain in the garden. Here are just a few that you might want to try.

- *F. graeca* (with brownish-green, delicately patterned flowers) is one of the smaller species, as is *F. michailovskyi* (with dark purple flowers with yellow tips). Both make good pot plants, kept dry in summer.
- *F. imperialis* (crown imperial) is the tallest and most robust species. Growing from large bulbs that have a foxy smell, they can reach more than 1m/3ft tall, displaying a cluster of bells at the top of the stem, in shades of orange or yellow.
- *F. meleagris* (snake's-head fritillary) is excellent for naturalizing in grass; it bears white or purple blooms with a pretty, chequered pattern.
- *F. pallidiflora* reaches 40cm/16in tall. It does well in cool shade and has large, square-shouldered, pale green flowers.
- *F. persica*, another tall species, has a spire of many pendent, bell-shaped flowers. In *F.p.* 'Adiyaman' they are rich, velvety purple and in *F.p.* 'Ivory Bells' creamy green.

Creating a drift of snake's-head fritillary

Snake's-head fritillary (*Fritillaria meleagris*) is an elegant spring bulb with downward-facing blooms, held on thin stems 20–30cm/8–12in tall. It is the perfect size for growing in grass, and there is a subtle beauty to a drift of these graceful flowers emerging from the green sward. The flowers can be purple, with a chequered pattern of paler marks, or white.

This bulb does best in soil that retains moisture year-round so you need to find a corner of your garden with damp but not waterlogged ground. This might be in a partially shaded corner under trees or in a shallow ditch or depression that never dries out completely.

It is also worth remembering that growing this bulb in grass means that you have to leave the grass uncut until the fritillary has died down for summer. If you have a space that fits these conditions and you do not mind letting the grass grow, then you can easily create a beautiful drift of these flowers.

The easiest way to plant small bulbs in grass is to lift a patch of the turf, place the bulbs on the soil underneath and replace the turf. Use a half-moon edger, if you have one, or a spade to cut through the grass on three sides of a square. Fold back the turf to expose the soil. Lightly fork over the ground before positioning the bulbs and then carefully fold back the turf over the bulbs. If you have a lot of bulbs to plant, cut several patches of turf close to each other. Once the bulbs start to grow, they will easily push through the grass to flower in mid-spring.

1. Handle the small bulbs of snake's-head fritillary carefully as they are fragile.
2. Cut three sides of a square in the grass with a spade or half-moon edger and fold back the turf.
3. Plant the small bulbs on the exposed soil.
4. Fold back the turf carefully and pat down gently to settle the grass back in. If you have more bulbs, cut another square of turf close by, to create a larger patch of flowers.
5. In spring, snake's-head fritillary blooms. A mixture of purple- and white-flowered forms looks very effective.

Snowdrop

Galanthus aka milk flower, Candlemas bells

More than any other flower, the snowdrop has come to symbolize the approach of spring in the garden. The small, pure white, pendent blooms look delicate, but these are tough plants, withstanding the worst of winter's wrath.

—

WHERE TO GROW
Snowdrops can be grown in most places that are not hot and dry in summer. They do best with a little moisture in the soil year-round and some cool summer shade. Under deciduous trees is ideal, as is naturalized in a lawn.

HOW TO GROW
Bulbs can be bought in autumn and are best planted straightaway so they do not become desiccated. Plant in clumps or small drifts, which will naturally increase over time. If flowering becomes erratic, it is time to divide the clump and spread out the plants.

GROWING TIP
Bulbs can be killed if kept too dry when dormant. To avoid this, snowdrops are often sold 'in the green', meaning they are dug up while still in growth. They can be planted like this in early spring.

Family	Amaryllidaceae
Height	10–20cm/4–8in
Flowering time	Winter
Hardiness	Zone 6
Position	Cool and partial shade

NOTABLE SPECIES AND CULTIVARS

- *G. nivalis* (common snowdrop) is an easy plant to grow and a good one to start with.
- *G. elwesii* is another easy species but taller than common snowdrop and with grey-green leaves.
- *G. woronowii* has shiny, bright green leaves and small, dainty flowers. It comes from the Caucasus and needs a little more moisture than other species.
- *G.* 'Atkinsii', *G.* 'Magnet' and *G.* 'S. Arnott' are among reliable cultivars.
- Double forms of common snowdrop are called *G. nivalis* 'Flore Pleno', but many other named double forms are available.

Galanthus elwesii

GALANTHOPHILIA
People fascinated by
snowdrops are called
Galanthophiles. They hold
snowdrop parties in winter,
showing off the variety of
forms they grow.

FLORAL VARIATION
The simple-looking flower of a
snowdrop is made up of three
outer petals and three smaller,
inner petals. On the inner petals,
and sometimes on the outer,
there are green markings. These
markings vary hugely and this,
combined with differences in the
leaves, flower size, stature and
flowering time, has resulted in
many hundreds of different forms
being named.

Gladiolus

Gladiolus aka sword lily

The large, showy cultivars of gladiolus make great summer flowers but they are not reliably hardy. There are a few species that will survive a winter outside, including magenta-pink *G. × byzantinus* and pale yellow *G. tristis*.

—

WHERE TO GROW
Even the tougher species of gladiolus need protection from hard frosts so are best grown in a sunny, sheltered border, against a wall or in a city garden. For a one-year show, plant the corms in a border or cutting garden (see Making a cut-flower patch, page 94).

HOW TO GROW
Most gladiolus corms can be planted in spring and will flower in any sunny part in the garden. In autumn, dig them up and store somewhere frost-free for winter. Frost-hardy species can be planted in autumn.

GROWING TIP
The fans of gladiolus's sword-like leaves bring a dramatic touch to a border, but they die down by late summer so you will need something to fill the space or hide it from view.

Family Iridaceae
Height 100–150mm/40–60in
Flowering time Summer
Hardiness Zones 3–6
Position Sunny and sheltered

Gladiolus papilio

SWORDS AT DAWN
Gladiolus has also been called *xiphium*, which comes from the Greek word *xiphios*, meaning 'sword', and *gladiolus* is Latin for 'small sword', referring to the sword-like leaves in both cases.

Crimson flag lily

Hesperantha coccinea aka *Schizostylis coccinea*

This late summer-flowering, rhizomatous perennial produces its pink to scarlet, open cup-shaped blooms right through autumn, providing a late colour boost to the garden. *Hesperantha coccinea* 'Major' has deep magenta-red flowers that seem to glow in the evening light.

—

WHERE TO GROW

Crimson flag lily is suitable for a sunny border in gardens where hard frosts are rare. It can be planted in herbaceous or mixed borders and tolerates most soil types as long as it is not waterlogged.

HOW TO GROW

This is a semi-evergreen perennial and is normally purchased growing in a pot, to be planted in spring or early summer. It needs plenty of moisture when in growth.

GROWING TIP

It is a vigorous plant that will increase to form dense clumps of narrow leaves. These can be divided in spring, to spread around your garden or to give away to friends.

Family Iridaceae

Height
50–75cm/20–30in

Flowering time
Late summer to autumn

Hardiness
Zone 4

Position
Full sun

ROOT CAUSE
Unlike other species of *Hesperantha*, this species grows from rhizomes, not corms, and so used to be known under a different name: *Schizostylis coccinea*.

Amaryllis

Hippeastrum

These massive South American bulbs produce striking, trumpet-like flowers in a range of bright colours, held at the top of a thick, sturdy stem. Given warmth and water they will flower in winter, and the bulbs are often given as presents.

—

WHERE TO GROW

The popular amaryllis are tender bulbs so need to be grown indoors (see Planting tender bulbs in a pot, page 42). Place in the pot in a warm place and, once growth appears, move to a spot in good light but not direct sunlight.

HOW TO GROW

Plant large bulbs in late autumn, with at least half the bulb above the soil. Give some water to start them growing. Once the leaves appear, make sure the soil does not dry out.

GROWING TIP

To get your bulb to flower again, it needs a cool, dark, dry period in late summer. In late autumn, bring back into the light and start watering again.

Family Amaryllidaceae	
Height 50–75cm/20–30in	
Flowering time Winter	
Hardiness Zone 2	
Position Light and warm	

NAME CONFUSION

The plants now known as *Hippeastrum* were previously in *Amaryllis,* hence the common name. True *Amaryllis* is a South African bulb with one species *A. belladonna* (see page 33).

Hippeatrum cultivars

Hyacinthella

Hyacinthella

Hyacinthella is a genus of small, rarely grown bulbs. Short racemes of little, bell-shaped flowers appear from between the rosette of leaves. The best species, such as *H. dalmatica* or *H. glabrescens*, have flowers in shades of blue or violet.

—

WHERE TO GROW

The various species of *Hyacinthella* will be lost in a garden border so are best grown in pots, a cold frame or raised bed, where they can be admired close up.

HOW TO GROW

Plant or pot the bulbs in autumn in free-draining soil. Keep the soil moist throughout winter and spring, but allow it to dry out once the plant has died back for summer.

GROWING TIP

If grown in a pot, top the soil with a layer of grit. This prevents wet soil splashing the plants and helps to keep excess water away from the leaves.

Family Asparagaceae

Height
5–10cm/2–4in

Flowering time
Spring

Hardiness
Zone 6

Position
Sunny and well-drained

GOOD COMPANY
Hyacinthella species come from south-east Europe and Turkey and are related to the well-known and popular hyacinth (see page 81).

Hyacinthella nervosa

77

Planting bulbs in a shady border

As you look through this book you will soon realize
that many bulbs need plenty of sunlight but if you have
a shady garden do not despair – there are plenty of bulbs
that can be grown under the dappled shade of deciduous
trees. These bulbs usually grow and flower in spring,
taking advantage of the light and moisture before the
trees grow their new leaves.

Shade-tolerant bulbs are often called woodland bulbs
and they include blue squills such as *Scilla bithynica*,
bluebells (*Hyacinthoides*), some cyclamen and fritillaries,
snowdrops (*Galanthus*) and dog's-tooth violets
(*Erythronium*). Dog's-tooth violets are elegant plants,
with flowers that have swept-back petals. They are the
perfect woodland bulb, thriving in humus-rich soil and
cool, partial shade (see also page 65).

Plant spring woodland bulbs in autumn. Find an
appropriate cool, shady spot, clear away the fallen leaves
and scatter a mixture of different bulbs over the ground.
Plant them where they land, digging deep enough so that
the bulbs are buried to a depth of two or three times their
size. Replace the soil and lightly firm.

Lilies flower in summer, and many of them can grow
in partial shade. Turk's cap lily (*Lilium martagon*)
flowers in early summer. It can reach more than 1m/3ft
tall, so will appear above other woodland plants,
displaying several flowers on a stem. These are normally
a shade of pink or purple, and there is also a white form.
Much taller and also suited to woodland conditions is
L. henryi. Flowering in mid- to late summer, this lily has
bright orange flowers and can reach 2m/7ft tall.

Lily bulbs are usually available from autumn through
to early spring, but it is best to plant them as early as
possible so the bulbs do not become desiccated while out
of the ground. Plant them in loose clumps or scatter them
randomly through other plants.

1. The bulbs of dog's-tooth violet are long and thin, like a canine tooth.
2. Plant the bulbs of dog's-tooth violet in holes dug with a trowel. The depth of the hole should be at least three times the size of the bulb.
3. Yellow dog's-tooth violets such as *Erythronium* 'Pagoda' look great with blue squills (*Scilla*).
4. Diminutive European dog's-tooth violet (*Erythronium dens-canis*) looks good when flowering alongside yellow spring fumewort (*Corydalis solida*) in a woodland border.
5. A lily bulb has the loose scales attached only at the base. Once you have your bulbs, plant them as soon as you can so they do not dry out too much while out of the ground.
6. Orange-flowered *Lilium henryi* towers above other perennials in summer. It can cope with plenty of sunshine or dappled shade.

Bluebell

Hyacinthoides

The sight of a woodland floor covered in wild bluebells (*H. non-scripta*) is a glorious sight. The deep blue, tubular flowers hang from the arching stem. Spanish bluebell (*H. hispanica*) has paler blue flowers and is more upright.

—

WHERE TO GROW

Bluebells are woodland plants, flowering just as the leaves appear on the trees. In the garden, they need moist soil and dappled shade. Spanish bluebells are more tolerant of sun and summer drought.

HOW TO GROW

Plant bulbs in early autumn, as soon as you get them. Never dig up wild plants. Group together in a partially shady corner, and they will start to multiply over time. Spanish bluebell is more vigorous and will soon spread.

GROWING TIP

Bluebells look great in their natural setting but can take over a small garden, especially Spanish bluebells. Remove seed pods before they split open, to keep under control.

Family	Asparagaceae
Height	30–40cm/12–16in
Flowering time	Spring
Hardiness	Zone 6
Position	Full sun to partial shade

Hyacinthoides non-scripta

HYBRID VIGOUR

English and Spanish bluebells hybridize to make a plant even more vigorous than either parent. This hydrid can be invasive and has been known to contaminate wild populations of English bluebells.

Hyacinth
Hyacinthus orientalis

The intoxicating scent and range of colours, from white and yellow to candy-pink, blue and purple, have ensured hyacinths are among the most popular spring bulbs. Although often enjoyed indoors, they are equally happy when planted in the garden.

—

WHERE TO GROW
In the garden, grow hyacinths in a sunny border with good drainage, or else in a cut-flower spot (see Making a cut-flower patch, page 94). Bulbs that have been grown indoors can be planted outside once their leaves have died down and they will continue to flower every spring.

HOW TO GROW
Hyacinths sold in containers usually have the top of the bulb showing, but when planting in the garden they should be buried with at least 5cm/2in of soil above them.

GROWING TIP
If you are finding it difficult to find the right place for these uniform, rigid flowers in your garden, you can replant the bulbs in a pot. They go well with daffodils (*Narcissus*) or early tulips, to make a container filled with spring colour.

Family Asparagaceae	
Height 15–20cm/6–8in	
Flowering time Spring	
Hardiness Zone 4	
Position Sunny and well-drained	

TURKISH DELIGHT
Wild hyacinth (*Hyacinthus orientalis*) is rarely seen in cultivation. It comes from southern Turkey and is the origin of today's colourful cultivars.

81

Spring starflower

Ipheion uniflorum aka *Tristagma uniflorum*, springstar

The pretty, star-shaped blooms of low-growing spring starflower are usually a shade of blue, ranging from soft pale blue to deep violet-blue. Also look out for white-flowered *I.* 'Alberto Castillo' and pink-flowered *I. uniflorum* 'Charlotte Bishop'.

—

WHERE TO GROW

Spring starflowers are hardy but the early flowers and leaves can be damaged by a late frost, so a sunny, sheltered position is best. They also make good bulbs for a pot – the starry flowers being held just above the long, narrow leaves.

HOW TO GROW

Plant bulbs in autumn in a border or a pot. They will struggle in heavy clay, preferring moist but free-draining soil. They should not dry out completely in summer.

GROWING TIP

For the best effect, plant bulbs in groups rather than spread out through a border. Individually, the plants can be insignificant, but when planted together they make an attractive early spring display.

Family	Amaryllidaceae
Height	10–15cm/4–6in
Flowering time	Spring
Hardiness	Zone 5
Position	Sunny and sheltered

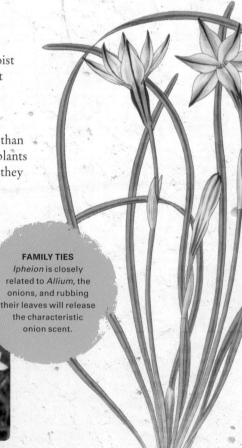

FAMILY TIES
Ipheion is closely related to *Allium*, the onions, and rubbing their leaves will release the characteristic onion scent.

Iris

Iris aka reticulate iris, Spanish iris, Dutch iris, early bulbous iris

Hugely varied but easily recognizable, irises come in a wonderful array of colours. There is an iris for almost any garden situation: the tallest growing from thick rhizomes, and the smallest growing from bulbs and flowering in late winter. The bulbous Dutch and Spanish irises flower from mid- to late spring.

—

WHERE TO GROW

All bulbous irises need sunshine and free-draining soil and there are plenty that are perfect for a raised bed or sunny border. The winter-flowering reticulate irises are especially good in pots and, when given some protection from winter weather, will flower very early in the year.

HOW TO GROW

Iris bulbs can be bought in autumn and planted in a light, sunny spot in the garden or in pots. The short, winter-flowering irises such as *I. reticulata* benefit from a mulch of grit, to keep wet soil away from the flowers.

GROWING TIP

Iris reticulata and its cultivars are more likely to flower in subsequent years if they are planted at least 10cm/4in deep. Shallower planting often leads to the bulbs splitting and producing only leaves after the first year.

Family	Iridaceae
Height	10–60cm/4–24in
Flowering time	Winter to spring
Hardiness	Zone 5
Position	Sunny and well-drained

Iris xiphium

RAINBOW FLOWERS
Iris is named after the Greek goddess of the rainbow, reflecting the range of colours found in the flowers of these beautiful plants.

African corn lily

Ixia aka corn lily, wandflower

African corn lilies are striking plants, with narrow foliage and
spikes of starry flowers, often each with a dark central blotch.
Colours range from bright red and pink to orange, yellow and
white, but the most amazing is the stunning, turquoise-green
I. viridiflora.

—

WHERE TO GROW

African corn lilies need a sunny, sheltered garden, near the
coast or in a city, where hard frosts are rare. They flower in
early summer. They are often grown in pots, and protected
from the cold in winter.

HOW TO GROW

Plant corms in autumn, in light, sandy soil and full sun.
Water well when in growth, but good drainage is important as
African corn lilies need to be as dry as possible when dormant.

GROWING TIP

You are more likely to have success with these bulbs if
you grow them in very gritty, loam-based soil in a pot.
Keep the pot protected from frost in winter and
allow the soil to dry out completely in summer.

Family	Iridaceae
Height	30–50cm/12–20in
Flowering time	Early summer
Hardiness	Zone 4
Position	Sunny and sheltered

Ixia polystachya

BEETLE JUICE
Some African corn
lilies are pollinated
by beetles. The dark
central markings and a
lack of scent are typical
of beetle-pollinated
flowers.

Cape cowslip

Lachenalia

Although hugely variable in the wild, relatively few of the more than a hundred species of Cape cowslips are in general cultivation. Those that are available are wonderful plants, often with spotted or striped leaves arranged around an erect spike of colourful, tubular flowers.

—

WHERE TO GROW

Coming from southern Africa, almost all Cape cowslips need protection from frost so need a very sheltered garden. It is better to grow them in pots that are protected from the cold and taken outside in spring. Pots should not be kept inside year-round because too much warmth can reduce flowering.

HOW TO GROW

In late autumn, plant bulbs in free-draining soil. Water well when in growth. Once dormant, allow the soil to dry out.

GROWING TIP

Plant the bulbs close to each other in a pot but not touching. They often flower better when crowded together.

MISLEADING NAME
The common name is confusing as these plants are nothing like the common cowslip (*Primula veris*). They are more like hyacinths and are in the same family.

Family Asparagaceae

Height
15–30cm/6–12in

Flowering time
Early spring

Hardiness
Zone 2

Position
Sunny and sheltered

Lachenalia quadricolor

Designing a spring bulb extravaganza

You can create a fantastic spring garden just using bulbs. If you have a bare patch of ground or some empty pots, you can fill them with colour from late winter to the beginning of summer. There is such a huge variety of spring-flowering bulbs that you can use them just on their own or mix them with spring bedding plants such as pansies (*Viola × wittrockiana*), polyanthus (*Primula* Polyanthus Group) and wallflowers (*Erysimum*).

For early-season flowers, plant crocuses and early daffodils such as *Narcissus* 'Tête-à-tête' or *N.* 'February Gold'. These will soon be followed or joined by glory of the snow (*Scilla luciliae*) and squills such as *S. siberica*.

The main colour in mid-spring is provided by daffodils, tulips and hyacinths. Crown imperials (*Fritillaria imperialis*) will also go well with spring bedding plants and smaller bulbs. Small bulbs include grape hyacinths (*Muscari*) and anemones. You can combine these to create a stunning display. To see the best examples of this type of planting, you should visit the amazing Keukenhof garden in the Netherlands. Open for only a few weeks in spring, this garden will dazzle you as well as give plenty of inspiration.

Before planting bulbs in your garden, the first thing to do is prepare the ground in autumn by digging it over and removing weeds. Then place the bulbs to form the pattern you want, and plant them using a trowel to dig individual holes. If you are using bedding plants as well, plant these first and arrange the bulbs among them.

Whether you plant your bulbs in the ground or in pots, at the end of spring you should dig them up and replace with something else for summer. The bulbs you have removed can be planted elsewhere, in a less formal part of the garden. By autumn, you can start planning a new display, using fresh bulbs.

1 An early spring display of Dutch hybrid crocuses and lady tulips (*Tulipa clusiana*).
2 This densely planted display is from the Keukenhof garden in the Netherlands. *Anemone blanda* 'White Splendour' surrounds tulips. In the background, blue grape hyacinths (*Muscari*) form an edge to a bed of mixed double tulips.
3 A mid-spring display of *Narcissus* 'Jack Snipe' and *N.* 'Little Witch' and tulips, including pink *Tulipa* 'Beauty Queen' and *T.* 'Golden Apeldoorn'.
4 Planting spring bulbs in containers such as these terracotta pots can create a display just as good as bulbs planted in the ground.
5 Dark purple polyanthus (*Primula* Polyanthus Group) look eye-catching when planted with pink tulips, in containers at the Royal Botanic Gardens, Kew.

Glory of the sun

Leucocoryne

These beautiful spring bulbs produce a tall, very thin, leafless stem holding a loose umbel of shallowly saucer-shaped flowers, with rounded, spreading petals in white, blue or purple, sometimes with yellow or purple centres.

WHERE TO GROW

Coming from the semi-desert or summer-dry regions of Chile, glory of the sun needs a warm, sunny position, with little or no frost and well-drained soil. It is usually grown in a pot but can survive outside in a city or sheltered courtyard garden.

HOW TO GROW

Plant bulbs in gritty or sandy soil and protect from frost over winter. After flowering, the narrow leaves die back, and the soil should then be kept dry until late autumn.

GROWING TIP

Glory of the snow needs as much light as possible during winter, so grow it in a pot on a sunny windowsill or in a conservatory, to protect from frost.

Family Amaryllidaceae	
Height 30–50cm/12–20in	
Flowering time Spring	
Hardiness Zone 2	
Position Sunny and sheltered	

Leucocoryne ixioides

DESERT FLOWER
The flowers of glory of the snow are part of the glorious spectacle that is the flowering Chilean desert. After spring rains, the desert becomes a sea of colour, and these bulbs can be found growing out of pure sand.

Snowflake

Leucojum aka spring snowflake, summer snowflake, Lodden lily

Summer snowflake (*L. aestivum*) is like a giant snowdrop (*Galanthus*) but the petals are all the same size, forming a hanging, bell-shaped flower. Spring snowflake (*Leucojum vernum*) is shorter. Both species have green or yellow spots on the petal tips, and both flower in spring.

WHERE TO GROW
Snowflakes can be grown in a sunny, herbaceous or mixed border, with moisture-retentive but well-drained soil, or in dappled shade under deciduous trees and shrubs.

HOW TO GROW
These are easy bulbs to grow in soil that does not dry out completely in summer, much like snowdrops. Summer snowflake can be quite vigorous, although not invasive, and will form healthy, leafy clumps.

GROWING TIP
Plant the smaller spring snowflakes near the front of a border, but the summer snowflake can hold its own with taller plants, and even does well alongside a stream, in moist but not waterlogged soil.

Family	Amaryllidaceae
Height	20–50cm/8–20in
Flowering time	Spring
Hardiness	Zone 6
Position	Sun or partial shade

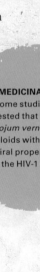
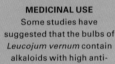

Leucojum vernum

MEDICINAL USE
Some studies have suggested that the bulbs of *Leucojum vernum* contain alkaloids with high anti-retroviral properties against the HIV-1 virus.

Lily

Lilium

The large, colourful flowers, often scented and appearing in the middle of summer, have ensured lilies are among the most popular bulbs for the garden. Their vibrant blooms can compete with the most flamboyant summer perennials, and in some forms can be held 2m/7ft above ground.

—

WHERE TO GROW

Lilies need moisture in summer and can be grown with herbaceous perennials in a sunny or partially shaded border, or under trees, in humus-rich soil that is never waterlogged. Lilies are also great in large pots, displayed on a patio.

HOW TO GROW

Prepare the soil before planting the bulbs, by digging in leafmould or garden compost; this will retain help moisture but allow good drainage (see also Planting bulbs in a shady border, page 78). Some lilies, particularly the oriental hybrids, need acid soil so check before buying.

GROWING TIP

Lily bulbs are available all winter and are often sold with other summer bulbs in spring, but it is best to plant them in late autumn if you can. This prevents them drying out too much while out of the ground.

Family Liliaceae
Height 50–200cm/20–80in
Flowering time Summer
Hardiness Zone 6
Position Sun or partial shade

SPOT THE BULB
Lilies are found across the northern hemisphere and are hugely varied. One feature that unites them is the bulb, which is made up of loose scales, attached only at the base. This makes lily bulbs very recognizable (see page 79).

Lilium martagon

Lilium henryi

NOTABLE SPECIES AND CULTIVARS

- *L. regale* (regal lily) is one of the most spectacular species lilies. This Chinese native bears glistening, white trumpets flushed with reddish-purple on the outside and with yellow throats; these are held aloft on tall, leafy stems 1m/3ft or more in height.
- Lilies with flowers that have recurved petals are often called Turk's caps, and they include *L. henryi* and *L. davidii*. Both have nodding, orange flowers with darker spots towards the centres and anthers held out on long filaments.
- *L. martagon* is one of the easiest lilies for the garden. The leaves are held in whorls on a stem that carries several small Turk's cap flowers. Colours range from deep plum-purple to pale lilac and white.
- Asiatic lilies are easy to grow and have large, star-like flowers in many different colours. Some have been bred to produce outward- or upward-facing flowers. Short-stemmed forms are best for pots.
- Trumpet lilies are like regal lilies but come in many colours, from deep purple to yellow, orange and red. They can grow in acid or alkaline soil and make fine plants for a large container.
- The oriental hybrids flower towards the end of summer and have fragrant blooms. They will do best in acid soil. Their flowers may be trumpet- or saucer-shaped or large Turk's caps.

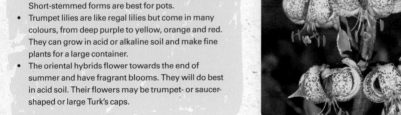

Nomocharis

Lilium pardanthinum aka *Nomocharis pardanthina*

This Chinese lily has beautiful flowers in pale pink or white, heavily spotted with darker pink and with frilly edges to the petals. Distinctive enough to originally be given its own genus (*Nomocharis*), it is now included within *Lilium* but often sold under the old name. *Lilium apertum* (aka *Nomocharis aperta*) is similar, but with darker pink flowers.

—

WHERE TO GROW
Nomocharis needs a cool, partly shady garden, acid soil and plenty of moisture in summer. It does best under trees or in the partial shade of a building; it does not do well in pots.

HOW TO GROW
Plant the small bulbs from late autumn to early spring, in humus-rich, moist but not waterlogged soil that does not dry out in summer.

GROWING TIP
If you can grow rhododendrons or other acid-loving woodland plants, then nomocharis should do well in your garden.

Family Liliaceae

Height
30–90cm/12–36in

Flowering time
Summer

Hardiness
Zone 6

Position
Cool and partial shade

RARE TREAT
Nomocharis can sometimes be seen in woodland gardens or displayed by specialist nurseries at flower shows. You might need to search it out to buy, but if you have the right conditions it is worth the effort.

Moraea

Moraea

The African genus *Moraea* contains many beautiful, iris-like species and they can be winter- or summer-growing, depending on where they occur in the wild. Those that are best for the garden are the summer-growing species such as tall, bright yellow *M. huttonii*.

Family Iridaceae

Height
50–70cm/20–28in

Flowering time
Summer

Hardiness
Zone 3

Position
Sunny and sheltered

WHERE TO GROW
The summer-growing species are the hardiest but still need a sheltered garden, in full sun. They do well on a rock garden or in a raised bed in regions where hard frosts are rare.

Moraea huttonii

HOW TO GROW
Plant corms of the summer growers in early spring, in free-draining, gritty or sandy soil. They need plenty of water in growth, but once the leaves have died back the corms should be kept on the dry side over winter.

GROWING TIP
If you are growing moraeas in a garden that has frequent frosts, protect the corms with a mulch over the soil, or keep them in pots in a cool greenhouse or conservatory.

BOTANICAL EYE
Moraeas look very similar to irises but with subtle differences in flower structure that only a botanist would notice; also, they grow from a corm, not a bulb.

Making a cut-flower patch

Some bulbs make great cut flowers, but you might not want to spoil the display in your garden by removing the flowers just as they are about to open. To keep your garden looking beautiful and bring some colour into your house, why not plant some bulbs specially for cutting?

You will need to find part of your garden that you do not mind using as a cut-flower patch. This does not have to be a large area, just enough for a few rows of bulbs. Clear the ground and dig it over to open up the soil and improve drainage. If you have heavy soil, dig in some garden compost to loosen it and help water to drain more easily.

Instead of digging a hole for each bulb, make planting easier by digging out a long, shallow trench. Mound up the soil on each side as you dig and plant the bulbs in a line along the bottom of the trench. Then push the soil back over the bulbs. Planting bulbs like this is similar to planting in a vegetable garden. After all, a row of onions is no different to a row of any other bulb. It is not unusual to grow cut flowers in a veg patch or allotment, and bulbs are no exception.

Choose a selection of bulbs that you can cut at different times. Daffodils (*Narcissus*), tulips and hyacinths all make colourful, long-lasting cut flowers. Cut the stems when they have buds; the flowers will soon open once in the warmth. For later flowers, plant gladioli or ornamental onions (*Allium*). These also last well once cut. Even after the flowers of ornamental onions have faded, the seed heads make a striking display, and can look rather like a bunch of miniature fireworks exploding in a vase.

1 Plant bulbs for cut flowers in rows, to make it easier. Any small area is enough to grow a good selection – you do not need a patch of ground this large.
2 Place the bulbs, such as these tulips, quite close together. There is no need to space them out, as you will be cutting the stems as soon as the buds appear.
3 Daffodils are among the earliest spring bulbs to bloom and make a great cut flower, bringing a little bit of spring into your home.
4 The later-flowering tulips such as this double-flowered *Tulipa* 'Drumline' have tall, upright stems in the garden, but once in a vase they can bend, making a wonderfully fluid arrangement.
5 A small patch of ground can still give you plenty of flowers to cut for the house.

Grape hyacinth

Muscari

Popular and easy to grow, these little spring bulbs produce a cluster of small, rounded flowers, looking just like a bunch of grapes. They are nearly always a shade of blue, but there are white and pink forms as well. The leaves are mostly long, thin and floppy.

—

WHERE TO GROW

Grape hyacinths are suitable for most gardens, under shrubs or spread through a border, even in grass.

HOW TO GROW

Most grape hyacinths are hardy, tough and easy to please – just avoid waterlogged soil and deep shade. Plant in autumn and leave them to it.

GROWING TIP

The most vigorous forms such as *M. armeniacum* can become a nuisance in the wrong place, but are perfect for mass planting, covering the ground under shrubs or along a hedge.

Family	Asparagaceae
Height	10–20cm/4–8in
Flowering time	Spring
Hardiness	Zone 6
Position	Sun or partial shade

Muscari armeniacum

TOUCH OF CLASS
Most grape hyacinths have untidy foliage but there is one species, *M. latifolium*, that has a single, wide, upright leaf, creating an elegant backdrop to the little, blue flowers.

Daffodil

Narcissus aka narcissi, lent lily, pheasant eye

Think of spring and you think of daffodils. Their bright yellow flowers brighten the garden and signal that winter is over. A typical daffodil flower has six petals and a central trumpet, called the corona. They may be single-flowered or multi-headed, in yellow, white or even pale pink.

—

WHERE TO GROW

Daffodils can be grown in a border, at the base of a tree or in grass (see Designing a spring bulb extravaganza, page 86). They are very adaptable, and most are no trouble at all. Small cultivars and species can be grown in a raised bed or in pots (see also Making a bulb lasagne, page 58).

HOW TO GROW

Plant bulbs 10–15cm/4–6in deep in early autumn. Scatter randomly through a border or group together in clusters. The small species such as *N. bulbocodium* need good drainage and an open position, where they will not be overcrowded by other plants.

GROWING TIP

After flowering, the leaves will last another few weeks. Some people tie the leaves in knots, but this can reduce photosynthesis and weaken the bulb. If growing daffodils in a lawn do not cut the grass until the leaves die down.

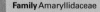

Family	Amaryllidaceae
Height	15–50cm/6–20in
Flowering time	Spring
Hardiness	Zone 6
Position	Sun or partial shade

GREEN FLOWER
The vast majority of daffodils flower in spring but a few of the species flower in autumn, including the bizarre, green-flowered *N. viridiflorus.*

Narcissus bulbocodium

*Narcissus
papyraceus*

DAFFODIL DIVISIONS

There are many, many daffodil cultivars and
to help make sense of them they are put in
different groups, called divisions, based on
the flower type. Some of the most popular
are the trumpet daffodils, such as yellow
N. 'Dutch Master' and white *N.* 'Mount Hood'.
These have a long corona and are what
most people think of as a typical daffodil.
The Large-cupped daffodils have a shorter
corona than the Trumpet Division, and the
Small-cupped daffodils have an even shorter
corona, less than a third of the length of the
petals. There are Double-flowered daffodils, in
which the corona is replaced with a bunch of
overlapping petals, and Split-corona daffodils
that have their corona cut over halfway into
segments that overlap the petals. Several
divisions are named after species. The Tazetta
daffodils, for example, are multi-flowered
like *N. tazetta* and include the early flowering,
strongly scented paper-white narcissus
(*N. papyraceus*). The widely grown, early
flowering *N.* 'February Gold' belongs to the
Cyclamineus Division, which have swept-back
petals like the species *N. cyclamineus*.

Nerine

Nerine bowdenii aka autumn lily

The fat shoots of nerine push through the ground in autumn and reach upwards as the flared trumpet-shaped flowers open at the top of the stem. *Nerine bowdenii* is the most commonly grown and has bright pink flowers. There are also white forms and deep cerise pinks, such as *N.b.* 'Isabel'.

—

WHERE TO GROW

Any open, sunny border is fine for *N. bowdenii*, which emerges as summer perennials fade to deliver some welcome autumn colour. In frost-prone gardens, a sheltered position is best, such as at the base of a wall, facing the sun.

HOW TO GROW

The leaves of nerine grow after the flower stems have appeared, and they last all winter. Plant new bulbs in spring just below soil level. They can take a year or two to get going, but once established they flower freely.

GROWING TIP

Nerine bowdenii is the hardiest nerine and does best when not overcrowded by other plants. The bulbs resent disturbance and often flower best once the bulbs themselves have become congested.

Family	Amaryllidaceae
Height	40–60cm/16–24in
Flowering time	Autumn
Hardiness	Zone 5
Position	Sunny and sheltered

NEW HOME
The half-hardy, South African *N. sarniensis* is called Guernsey lily or Jersey lily because it has become naturalized on the Channel Islands.

Star of Bethlehem

Ornithogalum aka chincherinchee

Many *Ornithogalum* species can be found wild in South Africa, but it is those from the Mediterranean region that are the most hardy and suitable for gardens. In spring, they produce bright, star-like, white flowers, backed with flashes of green.

—

WHERE TO GROW

Any sunny position suits star of Bethlehem, in a well-drained border or gravel garden. It can also be grown in light, dappled shade under trees or in grass.

HOW TO GROW

Hardy species of star of Bethlehem, such as *O. umbellatum* and the tall *O. nutans*, are easy to grow and happily spread through a border. Plant in autumn in free-draining soil.

GROWING TIP

Vigorous species such as *O. umbellatum* can spread rapidly by producing offsets and cover the ground with flowers but afterwards the foliage can look messy. Grow it with herbaceous perennials that will help to hide its leaves.

Family Asparagaceae	
Height 10–50cm/4–20in	
Flowering time Spring	
Hardiness Zone 6	
Position Sunny and well-drained	

Ornithogalum nutans

RISING STAR
Ornithogalum grows wild in western Asia so it is understandable why these little, white flowers appearing out of the ground, picked up the name 'star of Bethlehem'.

NOTABLE SOUTH AFRICAN SPECIES

- *O. candicans* (summer hyacinth or spire lily) has long been known as *Galtonia candicans*. It is one of the few South African species that is hardy enough to be grown outside, if temperatures do not fall below −10°C/14°F. It has many waxy, white bells arranged around a leafless stem that can reach 1.25m/4ft tall. A good clump will make an impact in a summer border. Plant the bulbs in early spring, in soil that retains moisture in summer but is well-drained. To improve drainage, add some grit under the bulb when planting or grow in large pots of free-draining soil.

The following species of *Ornithogalum* from South Africa need frost-free conditions and are better grown in pots or lifted and protected from freezing in winter.
- *O. dubium* (orange star flower) is one of the most striking, with large, deep orange blooms on stems to 30cm/12in tall.
- *O. saundersiae* (giant chincherinchee) grows more than 90cm/36in tall and has white flowers with a small, black ovary at the centre, held in a flat-topped flower head at the top of the stem.
- *O. thyrsoides* has a dense raceme of white flowers with pale green centres. It grows to 60cm/24in tall.

Ornithogalum candicans

Wood sorrel

Oxalis aka false shamrock

The best of this large group are fine plants such as
O. versicolor and *O. hirta*. They can have attractive leaves,
often divided into wide lobes, and funnel-shaped flowers
peering above the foliage. There are also some terrible
weeds in this genus, which should be avoided.

—

WHERE TO GROW

The best wood sorrels are mostly plants for a sheltered
position in a dry garden or raised bed. They are
also good pot plants, and the purple-leaved forms
of *O. triangularis* are perfect for a windowsill or
cool conservatory.

HOW TO GROW

Plant the bulbous wood sorrels in free-draining soil and
full sun. Some need frost-free conditions or at least some
shelter from the cold. Species that do well really in the
garden might become a pest.

GROWING TIP

Wood sorrel sold alongside other spring bulbs
are unlikely to be a problem, but if you buy
or are given a plant from another source
make sure it is not an invasive species.

Family Oxalidaceae

Height
10–20cm/4–8in

Flowering time
All seasons

Hardiness
Zone 3

Position
Full sun

Oxalis versicolor

PROBLEM PLANT
Some wood sorrels have
fibrous roots, and the
creeping wood sorrel
O. corniculata is a familiar
weed of gardens that is
almost impossible
to eradicate.

Growing bulbs from seed

It is hugely rewarding growing bulbs from seed, but it can take a long time for your seedlings to reach flowering size – this just makes it all the more satisfying when they do. Most bulbs will flower in about three years from sowing the seed, but some take longer. Sowing seed is the best way to get lots of new bulbs.

Crocus, tulip species, ornamental onions (*Allium*) and fritillaries are among the easier ones to try first but most bulbs should not be a problem; you just need patience. The first thing to do is collect some seed from bulbs in your garden. Keep an eye on your flowering bulbs once they have formed seed capsules. These will dry and split open to reveal the seeds. If you miss them, they will fall to the ground and you will not find them. Collect the seeds in an envelope or paper bag and keep dry.

The best time to sow your seed is around the same time the parent bulbs start back into growth after their dormant period. For spring bulbs, this will be in autumn or early winter; and for summer bulbs sow in late winter or early spring. It may be several weeks before you see the first leaf emerging.

The most important advice is to not disturb your seedlings after germination. Most bulb seedlings look like thin, grassy leaves. Leave them in the pot for at least a year before tipping them out. This gives them time to grow a little bulb. Do not let the soil dry out completely, even when the seedlings are dormant. If the seedlings look strong, they will probably each have formed their bulb and, once dormant again, you can pot them on into a larger pot and grow them on for another year or two, before transferring them to the garden.

1. Collect bulb seeds by gently breaking open the dried seed pod so the seeds fall out into your hand or a paper bag.
2. Fill a small pot with gritty or sandy soil to within 2.5cm/1in of the rim and sprinkle the seeds on to the surface.
3. Once the seeds have been sown, thinly cover them with some sieved soil.
4. Cover the soil surface with a thin layer of small gravel. This protects the soil from rain splashes that could disturb the seeds. Finally water the pot by standing in a tray of water.
5. Germinated bulb seeds such as from this lady tulip (*Tulipa clusiana*) develop thin, grass-like leaves.
6. Like most bulbs, lady tulip will flower three to five years after germinating,

Striped squill

Puschkinia scilloides

This is a short, pretty, little bulb, very like a small squill (*Scilla*) but displaying a spike of ice-blue flowers with a darker blue stripe down the centre of each petal. In the middle of each flower is a small, cup-like corona surrounding the anthers.

—

WHERE TO GROW

Striped squill is a small plant, so to appreciate it fully it is best planted in a raised bed or at the front of a border, in free-draining soil and full sun or partial shade.

HOW TO GROW

Plant bulbs in autumn, to create a drift of spring flowers, or put in a pot with taller bulbs such as daffodils (*Narcissus*) and tulips that flower at the same time.

GROWING TIP

Small bulbs such as those of striped squill are best planted in groups, as individually they are insignificant in a garden.

Family Asparagaceae

Height
10cm/4in

Flowering time
Spring

Hardiness
Zone 6

Position
Sun or partial shade and well-drained

TOUGH GUY
Sometimes the smallest plants are the toughest. Striped squill can grow at an altitude of up to 3,500m/10,500ft, in the mountains of eastern Turkey, flowering as the snow melts around it.

Star grass

Rhodohypoxis baurii aka *Hypoxis baurii*, red star

Star grass is a low-growing, clump-forming plant that flowers in summer with red, pink or white blooms at the centre of a rosette of narrow, hairy, pointed leaves. It creates an attractive carpet of colourful, starry flowers over several weeks.

—

WHERE TO GROW

Coming from the summer-rainfall areas of southern Africa, these plants want plenty of moisture when in growth but need to be kept relatively dry over winter, so plant them in a raised bed or grow them in a shallow pot.

HOW TO GROW

Plant the small, knobbly tubers near the soil surface, covered by a thin layer of soil. Drainage is really important because in winter star grass must not sit in damp ground.

GROWING TIP

If you grow star grass in a pot, move it to a cool greenhouse or cold frame for winter to keep dry. If planted outside where there is a lot of winter rain, cover plants with a sheet of glass or rigid plastic.

Family Hypoxidaceae

Height
10–15cm/4–6in

Flowering time
Summer

Hardiness
Zone 3

Position
Sunny and well-drained

WATER, WATER
Rhodohypoxis baurii comes from high altitudes in the Drakensburg Mountains of southern Africa and can be found growing in ground that is waterlogged in summer.

Mediterranean romulea

Romulea bulbocodium

This is the easiest and most widely available of the many species of *Romulea*. Looking like a spring crocus, the funnel-shaped flowers are lilac-purple, often with yellow throats, but they differ from crocuses in being held on a short stem among long, thread-like leaves.

—

WHERE TO GROW

Grow Mediterranean romulea in a warm, sunny position. It is perfect for a raised bed or rock garden, or in a sheltered gravel garden.

HOW TO GROW

Plant in autumn in well-drained soil. The small corms come into growth in winter and flower in spring, but need a sheltered position where frosts are not too severe.

GROWING TIP

The flowers of Mediterranean romulea need warmth to open wide and reveal their colourful petals, so plant them where they can make the most of any spring sunshine.

Family Iridaceae	
Height 10–20cm/4–8in	
Flowering time Spring	
Hardiness Zone 4	
Position Sunny and well-drained	

DISJUNCT DISTRIBUTION
The distribution pattern of *Romulea* species – with some found around the Mediterranean and the rest in southern Africa – is also seen in other bulbs such as star of Bethlehem (*Ornithogalum*) and gladiolus.

Roscoea

Roscoea aka hardy ginger

Roscoea is an unusual-looking plant, with intriguing, orchid-like flowers protruding from the top of a cluster of long, pointed leaves. Flowers are mostly purple or yellow, and different species can be in flower from late spring to late summer.

WHERE TO GROW
Coming from south-west China and the Himalaya, where summer rainfall is high, roscoea needs moist soil and some cool shade. Grow under trees or in a raised bed. Being dormant in winter, it is fully hardy if planted at least 10cm/4in deep in soil that does not freeze solid.

HOW TO GROW
Roscoea grows from a small rhizome with long, fleshy roots that should be planted in autumn, in moisture-retentive but free-draining soil. Water well in summer, and avoid ground that is very wet in winter.

GROWING TIP
Roscoeas can form healthy clumps over time, and it is beneficial to dig them up, carefully untangle the roots and spread them out, giving the plants more room and fresh soil.

Family	Zingiberaceae
Height	20–60cm/8–24in
Flowering time	Late spring to summer
Hardiness	Zone 5
Position	Partial shade

Roscoea humeana

NEW RED
In 1992, an Oxford University expedition to Nepal found a stunning, red-flowered form of *Roscoea purpurea*, a colour never seen before in the genus. It was named *R.p.* f. *rubra* and is still unique among cultivated roscoeas.

Squill

Scilla aka glory of the snow

There are few more wonderful sights in the early spring garden than a carpet of blue squills covering the ground beneath the trees. The genus *Scilla* contains many species, some reaching 60cm/24in tall or more, others hugging the ground; the majority flower in spring.

—

WHERE TO GROW

Small blue squills such as glory of the snow (*S. forbesii* and *S. luciliae*) can be planted under deciduous trees or in a lawn, where they will eventually cover the ground. Others such as Siberian squill (*S. siberica*) do best in a raised bed or rock garden.

HOW TO GROW

Most squills need free-draining but moisture-retentive soil. Plant with other early spring bulbs such as snowdrops (*Galanthus*) and winter aconite (*Eranthis hyemalis*).

GROWING TIP

Scatter the bulbs through a border in autumn and plant where they land, to create a natural effect. They will soon spread by themselves.

Family	Asparagaceae
Height	10–60cm/4–24in
Flowering time	Mostly spring
Hardiness	Zone 6
Position	Sun or partial shade

Scilla siberica

GLORY DAYS
Glory of the snow (*S. forbesii* and *S. luciliae*) used to be known as *Chionodoxa* and it is still sold under that name. You can recognize glory of the snow by the anthers held on triangular filaments, making a small, white cone at the centre of the flower.

Scilla bifolia

Scilla bifolia 'Rosea'

Scilla luciliae

NOTABLE SPECIES

- *S. bifolia* is one of the earliest to flower, with deep blue flowers on short stems.
- *S. bithynica* is one of the best squills for naturalizing. It is like a more robust and slightly later-flowering form of *S. bifolia* and will seed around prolifically in the right location, under dappled shade.
- *S. forbesii* (aka *Chionodoxa forbesii*) is also good for naturalizing, flowering just before *S. bithynica* and usually overlapping.
- *S. mischtschenkoana* is another early species. It has pale blue flowers that open close to the ground. It is slow to increase, but long-lived.
- *S. peruviana* is a larger species that is good for a garden border, deeply planted in well-drained soil. Despite its name, it comes from southern Europe, not Peru, and needs to be grown in full sun. It forms a rosette of pointed leaves and a wide, dense, domed flower head of typical blue squill flowers.
- *S. siberica* (Siberian squill) flowers in mid-spring and has amazing, intense blue flowers. It can be grown around shrubs or in a raised bed.

Winter daffodil

Sternbergia lutea aka fall daffodil

Large, golden goblets that emerge from the ground in autumn belong to the so-called winter daffodil, actually a species of *Sternbergia*. They flower at the same time as autumn meadow saffron (*Colchicum*), but have narrower, less imposing leaves.

—

WHERE TO GROW

Winter daffodil can easily be grown in a sunny, sheltered border, raised bed or rock garden. It does best in full sun and needs a warm, dry summer rest, so good drainage is important.

HOW TO GROW

Bulbs are sold in late summer and should be planted as soon as possible as, like *Colchicum*, they will soon start growing once in the ground.

GROWING TIP

Winter daffodil forms clumps that flower better the more congested they become. Newly planted bulbs may not flower straight away.

Family Amaryllidaceae	
Height 10–15cm/4–6in	
Flowering time Autumn	
Hardiness Zone 4	
Position Sunny and well-drained	

COUNT THE ANTHERS
Sternbergia is in the same family as daffodils (*Narcissus*) but looks more like a crocus. You can tell the difference by looking inside the flower, which has six anthers in *Sternbergia* and three in crocus.

Chilean blue crocus

Tecophilaea cyanocrocus aka Chilean crocus

One of the most stunning spring bulbs, the Chilean blue
crocus bears vivid, rich blue flowers, with white centres.
They are widely trumpet-shaped and held just above
the ground on thin stems. *Tecophilaea cyanocrocus*
'Leichtlinii' has paler blue flowers.

—

WHERE TO GROW

Despite coming from the Andes mountains of Chile, the
blue crocus is not reliably hardy and needs a dry summer
rest. In gardens where hard frosts are rare, it can be grown
in a raised bed or at the base of a sunny wall.

HOW TO GROW

Plant in autumn; the corms will then send up leaves
in winter, followed in early spring by flowers. Well-
drained soil is needed to keep excess moisture away
from the bulbs.

GROWING TIP

To protect the corms from hard frost, Chilean blue
crocus is often seen in alpine plant collections,
grown in pots in a cool greenhouse.

Family Tecophilaeaceae	
Height 10–15cm/4–6in	
Flowering time Early spring	
Hardiness Zone 3	
Position Sunny and sheltered	

BACK FROM THE BRINK

The desire to grow the striking
flowers led to over-collection of
Chilean blue crocus from the wild,
and for many years it was thought
to be extinct. Then in 2001 new
populations were discovered near
Santiago de Chile.

Naturalizing autumn bulbs in your garden

A bulb that is naturalized in the garden is one that, left alone, will increase naturally and colonize a border or lawn. This is either by setting seed that germinates and grows into new plants or by producing offsets or stolons from the parent bulb that result in a gradual increase in the number of plants.

The key to naturalizing bulbs is choosing the right ones. There are plenty of spring bulbs that can be naturalized but in autumn the choice is more limited. The three main autumn bulbs to choose from are the autumn species of *Crocus*, meadow saffron (*Colchicum*) and ivy-leaved cyclamen. They should be planted in late summer and can flower in just a few weeks.

One of the easiest autumn crocuses to grow is *Crocus speciosus*, which is usually violet-blue with delicate markings, but can also be white. Plant the corms in a lawn and they will flower in early autumn. At this point you should stop cutting the grass until spring. The crocus leaves grow after the flower and are thin and grass-like so disappear in a lawn.

Meadow saffron is often planted around a tree because they are kept dry under the canopy in summer. The early-autumn flowers are pink, violet or white. The bulbs naturally divide and more flowers will appear over time, slowly filling the space.

Ivy-leaved cyclamen (*Cyclamen hederifolium*) is the hardiest of all cyclamen and the flowers can appear from late summer. The round tubers should be planted near the soil surface in dappled shade or in grass. The flowers emerge from growing points on the top, held on thin stems before the leaves unfurl. This is a plant that in some gardens will happily survive but in others it will be incredibly vigorous, spreading by seed through borders and covering the ground with their attractively patterned leaves all winter.

1 *Crocus speciosus* is an autumn-flowering species that can be planted in a lawn, where it will slowly increase.
2 Meadow saffron planted under a tree is kept dry in summer before it comes to life in autumn and produces its large, goblet-shaped flowers.
3 Ivy-leaved cyclamen is a wonderful autumn flower, with attractive leaves that last all winter. It spreads by seed, colonizing a border in the right conditions.

Tiger flower

Tigridia pavonia aka peacock tiger flower, Aztec lily

Tiger flower is probably the most exotic-looking garden bulb, with its long, sword-shaped leaves and wide, gaudy summer flowers that come in a range of bright colours, from yellow and orange to pink and red. Individual flowers last only a few hours but several open in succession.

—

WHERE TO GROW
Tiger flower can be grown outside in gardens where frosts are rare, in a raised bed or dry garden with gravelly or sandy soil. Otherwise, they are good in pots, displayed in summer and protected from freezing in winter.

HOW TO GROW
Plant bulbs in spring, in full sun. If left in the ground over winter they will tolerate light frost, but if frosts are common or the soil is heavy it may be safer to lift the bulbs in autumn store them dry over winter.

GROWING TIP
Tiger flower is easy to grow from seed (see Growing bulbs from seed, page 104) and can flower in the first year if sown early enough, with some warmth, in a greenhouse or conservatory. Later sowings will produce flowers in the following year.

Family	Iridaceae
Height	30–50cm/12–20in
Flowering time	Summer
Hardiness	Zone 3
Position	Sunny and sheltered

AZTEC FOOD
The bulbs of tiger flower were a food for the Aztecs, who called them *cacomitl*. They apparently taste a little like sweet potato; however, never try eating newly bought bulbs, as they may have been treated with pesticide.

Wake robin

Trillium aka birthroot, American shamrock, American wood lily

Wake robin grows from a rhizome and flowers in spring.
It has a distinctive appearance with three large, rounded,
often mottled leaves surrounding a three-petalled flower.
This flower either sits directly on top of the leaves or has
a short stem.

—

WHERE TO GROW

These are woodland plants in the wild so need cool shade
and rich, deep, humus-rich soil, under deciduous trees
or in a partially shaded corner of the garden.

HOW TO GROW

The rhizomes, which are often sold along with bulbs, should
not dry out so plant them straightaway, 8–10cm/3–4in
deep. They can take a few years to establish and are slow
to increase.

GROWING TIP

Wake robin will not survive in heavy clay or
waterlogged soil, nor will it tolerate drying out
at any time. Improve your soil with garden
compost or well-rotted manure so that it retains
moisture but excess water drains freely.

Family	Melanthiaceae
Height	50cm/20in
Flowering time	Spring
Hardiness	Zone 5
Position	Cool and shady

Trillium grandiflorum

THREE-DIMENSIONAL
The 'tri' in *Trillium*
means triple and refers
to the parts of the plant
all being in threes.

Triplet lily

Triteleia laxa aka grass nut, Ithuriel's spear, florists' brodiaea

Triplet lily is best known as a cut flower, the florists' brodiaea, but is not a common garden plant, mainly because it is not reliably hardy. In the right place, it can be very attractive, with its bright purple-blue flowers held in a loose umbel in early summer.

—

WHERE TO GROW

Grow triplet lily in a warm, sunny part of the garden, sheltered from hard frost. It is ideally suited to a dry gravel garden or raised bed.

HOW TO GROW

Triplet lily is a winter-growing plant that flowers at the end of its growing season, once the leaves have died down. Plant dormant corms in autumn in light, well-drained, sandy soil.

GROWING TIP

To hide the leaves as they die back, grow triplet lily among low ornamental grasses or low-growing perennials.

Family Asparagaceae	
Height 30–50cm/12–20in	
Flowering time Early summer	
Hardiness Zone 3	
Position Sunny and well-drained	

FLORAL NAMES
The botanical names *Triteleia* and *Brodiaea* have both been used for triplet lily, which is why this plant, a good cut flower, is still sometimes called florists' brodiaea.

Tritonia

Tritonia disticha aka *Tritonia rosea, Crocosmia rosea*

These elegant South African corms are similar in appearance to African corn lily (*Ixia*) and montbretia (*Crocosmia*). They have long, narrow leaves and colourful flowers held on a tall, thin stem. There are several species but *Tritonia disticha* is among the few that are widely grown.

—

WHERE TO GROW

Tritonia needs plenty of sunlight and free-draining soil so plant the corms in a gravel garden, raised bed or open border. They will thrive in a bright corner of a city garden or courtyard.

HOW TO GROW

The corms are summer growing and should not be allowed to dry out completely at any time. Some of the leaves can persist over winter, but they are reasonably hardy and plants should survive light frosts.

GROWING TIP

If frosts are common, protect corms from freezing by covering with a thick, dry mulch in winter.

Family Iridaceae

Height
50–80cm/20–32in

Flowering time
Summer

Hardiness
Zone 4

Position
Sunny and well-drained

IN THE FAMILY
The iris family includes many plants from southern Africa. As well as *Tritonia*, there are *Crocosmia, Ixia, Dierama, Gladiolus, Moraea, Romulea* and *Watsonia*.

Planting a winter bulb garden

Winter-flowering bulbs bring life, colour and hope to a garden on the shortest, coldest days of the year. From snowdrops (*Galanthus*), winter aconites (*Eranthis hyemalis*) and *Cyclamen coum*, to irises and the first crocuses, there is a good selection of winter bulbs to choose from.

You can plant winter bulbs in a part of the garden visible from your window so you do not have to venture outside to enjoy them. They can be used under shrubs and trees and to complement the colourful stems of dogwoods (*Cornus*) or the pale pink flowers of winter viburnums. Many are small enough for a window box so there really is no reason not to grow a few. They are mostly planted in autumn, but you can buy snowdrops and winter aconite in spring as growing plants ready to be put straight out in the garden.

Everyone's favourite, the snowdrop, flowers in the middle of winter but they do not have to be grown in isolation. One of the joys of a winter garden is that you can still create some attractive combinations with a relatively small range of plants, and winter blooms seem extra precious simply because of their scarcity.

When planting a winter border, think about using a selection of different bulbs to work together. Winter aconite has yellow flowers close to the ground and can form a backdrop to taller bulbs. Plant it with snowdrops or paper-white daffodil (*Narcissus papyraceus*) that can flower from early winter. *Cyclamen coum* can spread to cover the ground with rounded leaves and a profusion of sugary pink blooms. It too goes very well with snowdrops.

You should also think about the succession of flowers over the winter. In cold weather, flowers can last several weeks but eventually the mid-winter bulbs give way to late winter and early spring flowers. *Iris reticulata* and *Crocus tommasinianus* both flower towards the end of winter and bring the planting on as the season progresses.

1 Plant different winter bulbs together: for example, snowdrops (top), crocuses (bottom) and *Iris reticulata* (right).
2 Snowdrops survive ice and snow to bloom in the depths of winter, and their flowers can last several weeks.
3 Snowdrops and winter aconites make a classic winter combination.
4 The flowers of winter aconites last into late winter, when they combine with the first blooms of *Crocus tommasinianus*.
5 A large, well-established patch of *Cyclamen coum* can create a wonderful winter sight that can compete with any of summer's offerings.

Flame flower

Tropaeolum speciosum aka Scottish flame flower, Perth weed, Chilean flame creeper

The wonderful, scarlet-red flame flower has long, thin, twining stems with small, lobed leaves and a profusion of bright flowers in summer. Each miniature, horn-shaped flower has five flared, notched petals and a long spur pointing behind.

—

WHERE TO GROW
Flame flower needs cool, partial shade and a humid atmosphere to do well. It will grow through hedges and up nearby shrubs.

HOW TO GROW
Plant the white rhizomes in sandy, leafy soil and give them plenty of water in summer. Allow them to grow through nearby plants.

GROWING TIP
Flame flower can be hard to establish in a garden so plant the rhizomes in a narrow trench about 15cm/6in deep and only partially cover. As the stems grow up, gradually fill in the trench to ground level.

Family	Tropaeolaceae
Height	3m/10ft (supported)
Flowering time	Summer
Hardiness	Zone 5
Position	Cool partial shade

GREAT SCOT
Often called the Scottish flame flower because it does well in cool, damp summers, it can even become a weed, hence another common name, Perth weed, named after the Scottish town.

Tropaeolum speciosum

NOTABLE SPECIES

The common nasturtium (*T. majus*) is an annual, but there are several other perennial species that grow from tubers or rhizomes.

- *T. azureum* is a beautiful, blue-flowered species. It grows and flowers in winter but needs protection from frosts below −5°C/23°F. It does well in a large pot and can climb to 1m/3ft tall.
- *T. polyphyllum* is an easily grown, trailing plant, with grey-blue leaves and fleshy stems. The yellow flowers appear in spring. Although the stems are frost hardy, plant the rhizomes up to 30cm/12in deep to protect them from freezing soil. This species looks best on a raised bed or rock garden, where the stems can hang down.
- *T. tricolor* is sometimes called the three-coloured nasturtium because each small, yellow flower is surrounded by a purple-tipped, red calyx with a red spur pointing behind. It has a long flowering season, from late winter to late spring, but needs protection from frost.
- *T. tuberosum* is a vigorous, summer-flowering species; it grows from large tubers that can reach more than 5cm/2in across. The stems can reach 3m/10ft if allowed to climb over a trellis or fence, and they produce orange flowers tipped with yellow. The stems are not hardy, but the buried tubers can survive outside in regions where temperatures do not fall below −5°C/23°F.

Tropaeolum tricolor

Society garlic

Tulbaghia

From neat clumps of long, linear leaves emerge several tall, leafless stems, each with a cluster of small, trumpet-like flowers. The most widely grown is *T. violacea* and there are a few cultivars including the variegated *T.v.* 'Silver Lace'.

—

WHERE TO GROW

Society garlic is very drought tolerant and long-flowering. It needs good light so plant in a gravel garden, raised bed or sheltered, sunny border. It also makes a great pot plant.

HOW TO GROW

The bulbs can retain some leaves year-round, and clumps can be divided in spring to increase your plants. They are not reliably hardy, so need some protection from hard frost.

GROWING TIP

Cutting off the faded flower stems will encourage new stems to grow. Society garlic can flower all summer long.

Family Amaryllidaceae

Height
30–50cm/12–20in

Flowering time
Summer

Hardiness
Zone 4

Position
Sunny and sheltered

Tulbaghia violacea

REPELLENT
As the common name society garlic suggests, the leaves smell of garlic, when crushed. The strong smell can act as an insect repellent on your skin and even keep moles out of your garden.

Tulip

Tulipa

For sheer flower power you cannot beat tulips. Whether in ranks of single colours in bedding or when mixed and scattered though a border, the colourful cup- or vase-shaped blooms of tulips bring vibrancy and elegance to spring planting (see Three months of tulips, page 128).

Family Liliaceae	
Height 20–80cm/8–32in	
Flowering time Spring	
Hardiness Zone 6	
Position Sunny and well-drained	

WHERE TO GROW

Tulips can be grown in most locations, given plenty of sunshine. They can grace a border, raised bed or gravel garden. Grow them in a country garden or a city garden. They are fantastic in pots displayed on a patio or in a window box (see also Making a bulb lasagne, page 58).

HOW TO GROW

It is best to grow tulips for one season and replace them with new bulbs the following autumn. The highly bred cultivars usually fade after their first year, but some are more persistent if grown in sandy, free-draining soil.

GROWING TIP

If you want to grow tulips that last more than a year, then give some of the species a try; these are often sold as 'botanical' tulips. They also need sun and free-draining soil but will come back into flower year after year.

Tulipa sylvestris

RENEWABLE ENERGY

Tulips grow from a true bulb (see page 10) but it is renewed every year. The plant uses all the energy from the bulb as it grows, and a new bulb forms before the plant dies down for the summer.

TULIP DIVISIONS

Like daffodils, tulip cultivars are classified in divisions, according to their flower type.

- Three of the divisions are named after species they most closely resemble: the Kaufmanniana, Greigii and Fosteriana groups. The Greigii Group, for example, contains tulips that have similarities to the species *T. greigii*, with widely flared, funnel-shaped flowers and leaves often with dark spots or stripes.

- There are single and double tulips, split into early and late-flowering groups. The Single Late Group contains the classic, tall cultivars with egg-shaped flowers, such as *T.* 'Queen of Night'.

- The Lily-flowered Group has tulips with elegant blooms with pointed petals, such as *T.* 'Ballerina' and *T.* 'Red Shine'.

- The Darwin Hybrid Group has some of the largest flowers and, along with the Lily-flowered Group, are the tulip cultivars most likely to persist in the garden.

- The species tulips are less flamboyant but have a charm of their own and may continue in the garden for many years. Some of the best for outdoor cultivation are *T. sylvestris*, *T. clusiana*, *T. praestans* and the scarlet-red, early-summer tulip *T. sprengeri*.

Tulipa greigii

Three months of tulips

Tulips are one of the highlights of spring, with their vibrant blooms in many different colours and varied shapes. If you choose the right cultivars you can have tulips flowering for more than three months. Plant them in a border for a continuous display as one tulip succeeds another or plant them in pots that you can move into a prominent position when the tulips flower.

Among the first tulips to flower in early spring are those that belong to the Kaufmanniana Group – sometimes called water lily tulips. These have funnel-shaped flowers and can be a single colour, such as bright red *T.* 'Showwinner' or orange-red *T.* 'Love Song'. Other Kaufmanniana Group tulips have yellow or white flowers with red markings inside and on the backs of the outer petals, as in *T.* 'Ancilla'.

Closely following are the Single Early Group, which have sturdy stems to about 35cm/15in tall. They include pink *T.* 'Apricot Beauty' and violet-purple *T.* 'Candy Prince'.

Most tulips flower in mid-spring, and now you are spoilt for choice. The Triumph Group is one of the largest tulip groups; plants are similar to Single Early tulips but slightly taller and a little later in flower. Darwin Hybrid tulips are taller still, to around 55cm/22in, and display huge blooms that open wide in the sun. *T.* 'Ivory Floradale' bears silky white flowers and *T.* 'Daydream' has yellow flowers that age to pale orange.

Also flowering mid-season are Lily-flowered tulips. These have elegant, slim blooms with pointed petals. They include the ever-popular *T.* 'Ballerina', *T.* 'White Triumphator' and *T.* 'China Pink', but there are many more to choose from.

Moving into late spring, the tulips of the Single Late Group begin to bloom. From egg-shaped buds open deeply bowl-shaped flowers. Plants can reach 70cm/28in tall and are often planted in formal bedding schemes. There are many colours, but dark purple *T.* 'Queen of Night' is an old favourite.

1 *T.* 'Love Song' is in the Kaufmanniana Group and among the first tulips to bloom. It is a great tulip to start off the season.

2 Mid-spring tulips include large-flowered, yellow to pale orange *T.* 'Daydream' in the Darwin Hybrid Group.

3 Lily-flowered tulips such as *T.* 'Ballerina' have elegant flowers with pointed petals, and they also flower in mid-spring. In light, sandy soil, they can survive for several years.

4 The Single Late tulips are among the last tulips to flower. They include old favourites such as *T.* 'Queen of Night', but are among the least likely to come back a second year.

5 When you plant a selection of tulips in pots, you can have stunning colour for three months from early to late spring. This is a display of double tulips flowering in mid-spring.

Bugle lily

Watsonia aka Cape bugle lily

Bugle lilies are striking South African plants with fans of sword-shaped leaves and tall, symmetrical spires of funnel-shaped flowers in red, pink, orange, yellow and white. Summer growers such as *W. pillansii* flower in autumn and winter growers such as *W. borbonica* bloom during spring.

WHERE TO GROW

Unfortunately, bugle lilies are barely hardy and need protection from frost. They are worth trying in a sheltered city or coastal garden, but are best overwintered in a frost-free greenhouse or conservatory.

HOW TO GROW

Plant corms in spring or autumn but they can have leaves year-round, so you may find them pot-grown for sale. Bring the pots outside for summer and place in a sunny spot.

GROWING TIP

If grown outside, plant the corms against a warm, sunny wall to provide some protection.

Family	Iridaceae
Height	60–125cm/24–50in
Flowering time	Spring or autumn
Hardiness	Zone 3
Position	Sunny and sheltered

Watsonia borbonica

ISLAND LIFE

Watsonia Tresco hybrids originated on the island of Tresco in the Isles of Scilly, off the south-west coast of England, where winters are mild enough for them to be grown outside.

Arum lily

Zantedeschia aethiopica aka calla lily

This lily produces large, glistening white spathes held on thick, strong stems, making it a good cut flower. It is also a dramatic garden plant, with clumps of large, arrow-shaped leaves surrounding the flowering stems. *Zantedeschia aethiopica* 'Crowborough' is a popular cultivar.

—

WHERE TO GROW
Plant in deep, moist soil and full sun. Arum lily can be grown in a border or beside a pond. In the wild in southern Africa, it thrives in swampy ground and ditches.

HOW TO GROW
The above-ground parts of arum lily are not very hardy so plant the thick rhizomes deep enough to avoid freezing; they should then survive frosty winters. In frost-free gardens or given some protection from frost, the leaves are evergreen.

GROWING TIP
After a frosty night, the leaves might look like boiled spinach but do not panic – the plants will survive and grow new leaves in spring as the weather warms.

Family Araceae

Height
60–100cm/24–40in

Flowering time
Summer

Hardiness
Zone 4

Position
Moist but sunny

FIRST ARRIVAL
Arum lily was one of the first plants to be introduced to Europe from the Cape of South Africa. It is known to have been grown in the Jardin des Plantes, Paris, in 1644.

Rain lily

Zephyranthes candida aka Peruvian swamp lily

These South American bulbs flower in autumn, producing a white, goblet-shaped bloom held on a stem that can reach 20cm/8in long. It is in summer that they have their short rest, spurred back into life by late-summer rain.

WHERE TO GROW
Rain lily needs a warm, dry summer so plant in well-drained soil in a sunny position, at the base of a wall, in a raised bed or in a gravel garden. It is also suitable for a pot.

HOW TO GROW
Apart from during summer, these bulbs need plenty of moisture. Plant them in late summer, water them in and they should start to grow quickly, although they might not flower in their first year.

GROWING TIP
The best advice is to leave these bulbs alone once established. If grown in a pot, they will flower better if the bulbs are allowed to become congested.

Family	Amaryllidaceae
Height	20–30cm/8–12in
Flowering time	Autumn
Hardiness	Zone 4
Position	Sunny and well-drained

RAINMAKER
There are about thirty species of rain lily and they tend to flower soon after rain in their natural habitats, hence the common name. Flowering time can be spring, summer or autumn, depending on the local weather conditions.

Seeing bulbs in the wild

Do you ever wonder where the bulbs you grow in your garden come from? Seeing them growing wild, their flowers pushing through the rough grass of a hillside meadow, scattered through a woodland or peering from a rocky outcrop, gives you a new insight into the way they live. You will understand the conditions they grow in and see the other plants that grow alongside them, and it is exciting just to come across them as you explore their natural habitat.

Bulbs are most commonly found in regions with a seasonally dry, Mediterranean-type climate. Prime bulb hunting areas include California, South Africa, Chile and the Mediterranean region itself. Visit in spring or autumn and you will find flowering bulbs.

If you live in Europe then head south, to southern Spain, Greece, Turkey or any of the Mediterranean islands. If you are used to holidaying in the heat of summer, you will be pleasantly surprised by the greenery and freshness of a Mediterranean spring. You will not have to look far to find bulbs. Coastal headlands, rocky slopes, the edge of an olive grove and even roadside verges are all worth exploring. If you are keen to see a wide variety, then there are places where bulbs are particularly diverse. The hills of Andalucía in Spain, for example, or the Peloponnese of Greece, the western coast of Turkey and the island of Crete are all hotspots for bulb hunting.

Around the Mediterranean, the bulbs you are most likely to spot include grape

Autumn-flowering *Crocus speciosus* in a meadow in the Caucasus mountains of Georgia.

hyacinths (*Muscari*), star of Bethlehem (*Ornithogalum*) and anemones, and, at higher altitudes, crocuses grow in grassy meadows. Nearly 90 per cent of wild daffodils (*Narcissus*) are found on the Iberian Peninsula, so head to Spain and Portugal if you want to see these species. At the eastern end of the region, in Greece and western Turkey, you are likely to come across fritillaries and maybe a few tulips.

Tulips have a wide natural range, from the Mediterranean region eastwards to Central Asia, and it is in the mountains of Central Asia that they are at their most diverse. A trip there is for the more adventurous traveller, but there are plenty of organized tours that focus on the flora of the region. The Caucasus region in Georgia, Armenia and Azerbaijan is another hotspot of floral

Cyclamen hederifolium growing out of a stone wall in Italy.

diversity, with tulips, cyclamen, irises, snowdrops (*Galanthus*) and crocuses among the bulbs growing there.

In the southern hemisphere, Chile and South Africa are both rich in bulbous species. The small town of Nieuwoudtville in South Africa is known as the bulb capital of the world, but bulbs can be seen throughout the summer-dry climate region, from Cape Town to the semi-desert south of Springbok, Northern Cape. Gladioli, African corn lilies (*Ixia*), moraeas and bugle lilies (*Watsonia*) are among the plants to look out for. Farther east in Eastern Cape, Lesotho and the Drakensberg mountains, the summer-wet climate is home to summer growers such as African lily

(*Agapanthus*) and summer hyacinth (*Ornithogalum candicans*).

Deciduous woodland habitats can also be seasonally dry as the trees take up a lot of water when they are in full leaf. Plants take advantage of the light and moisture from late autumn to spring when the trees are bare. The woods of eastern North America, especially in the Appalachian mountains, are home to beautiful spring bulbs. Trilliums and dog's-tooth violets (*Erythronium*) are among the plants to see here. In the woods of northern Europe, particularly in the UK, bluebells (*Hyacinthoides*) create a magical display in late spring, carpeting the floor with their vivid blue flowers.

Bulb conservation

With everything they need to grow contained in a tidy, drought-tolerant package, bulbs are easy to transport. When kept dry and reasonably cool, they can be shipped around the world in huge numbers. Most bulbs for the horticultural trade are grown in cultivation fields or plant nurseries, and this trade poses no threat to wild plants. However, for those that are less easily grown in large quantities or are slow to increase, wild bulbs are still collected.

If the collection of wild plants to sell could threaten wild populations, the trade is regulated to ensure that harvesting is sustainable. The Convention on International Trade in Endangered Species of Wild Fauna and Flora (CITES) sets quotas for the export of certain species. Bulbs such as snowdrops (*Galanthus*) and cyclamen are typical of popular plants that are threatened in the wild simply because there is such a high demand for them from gardeners.

One example of a project to protect populations of a wild bulb is the collaboration between the Royal Botanic Gardens, Kew, CITES and the authorities in Georgia to ensure the sustainable harvesting of a particular snowdrop, *G. woronowii*. Through surveys of natural populations and the monitoring of cultivation programmes, an export quota has been set to limit the trade. If you are lucky enough to find yourself on a wooded slope surrounded by thousands of

Galanthus woronowii being grown in Georgia, as a crop for export.

snowdrops, you might think digging a few up would have no detrimental effect, but when you realize that 15 million bulbs are legally exported from Georgia every year it is easy to understand how unregulated trade could soon damage populations of this plant in the wild.

Chilean blue crocus (*Tecophilaea cyanocrocus*) was so over-collected after its discovery in the nineteenth century that for many years it was thought to be extinct in the wild. Brilliant scarlet *Tulipa sprengeri* is still thought to be extinct, only surviving in cultivation because of its ability to produce large quantities of viable seed.

Thus, it is important to conserve wild plants and realize that even a low level of collecting can have an adverse effect on a plant's survival.

Troubleshooting

Most common garden bulbs are fairly resilient if grown in the right place, and serious problems are rare. Good cultivation is the key to keeping your bulbs healthy. If they seem weak or do not flower, or if they disappear after their first year, it is more than likely that poor growing conditions are the cause.

There are, of course, pests that will feed on the healthiest plants and, if left to get out of control, can eventually kill a bulb. The most common are insects that feed on the sap in juicy leaves and stems, weakening the plant and leaving it vulnerable to fungal infections. Sap-sucking insects can also spread virus. Other insects feed on the leaves themselves and can completely defoliate a plant, causing enough damage to fatally weaken the bulb. The most common problem for the bulb itself is fungal disease, but insects can feed on it, too.

DISAPPEARING BULBS

The most common reason for bulbs vanishing is unsuitable soil conditions. Many bulbs need a reasonably dry dormant period in summer, and if the soil remains wet year-round the bulbs can rot away, unless they need some moisture in summer, like the snake's-head fritillary (*Fritillaria meleagris*).

Soil compaction can be a problem for bulbs grown in a lawn. If the grass is heavily walked on, the soil will not drain as well as normal, leading to waterlogging. It is worth spiking your lawn in autumn with a garden fork, to aerate the soil. Brush in about 5mm/¼in sandy topsoil, to improve the drainage.

DWINDLING FLOWERS

If left to form congested clumps, individual bulbs will be starved of nutrients, sending up leaves but no flowers. Lift the clump, separate the bulbs and spread them out, giving each one room to grow and to access more nutrients in the soil. Snowdrops (*Galanthus*), for example, should be lifted and divided every few years.

Bulbs grown in pots can also suffer from a lack of nutrients. Always use fresh soil mix when planting up a new container (see Growing bulbs in pots, page 20). When the bulbs are growing, feed with low-nitrogen liquid fertilizer.

If pots are kept in a greenhouse or conservatory, the extra protection allows pests such as mealy bug to flourish. Usually found in bulbs quietly munching away on all that stored goodness, mealy bugs look like miniature woodlice or pill bugs, but are covered in white, powdery wax. Paint mealy bugs with methylated spirit to break down their waxy coating and kill them.

DISTORTED GROWTH

If the flower stem or leaves look distorted, you will probably find an infestation of aphids, also known as greenfly or blackfly. They multiply at an incredible rate and form a dense colony on young growth. They can smother a flower bud, causing it to abort, and also thrive on the undersides of leaves. Aphids excrete a sticky substance called honeydew, and ants love it. They will 'farm' the aphids, moving them around

The bright red adult lily beetle looks pretty, but its larvae can do a lot of damage.

or transferring them to new plants. The honeydew dripping on to leaves can also encourage sooty moulds to grow.

Aphids can be sprayed with insecticide but, with the help of the ants, they will be back so regular treatment is necessary. Alternatively, you can spray them with soapy water, which blocks their breathing pores but can also damage the plant if used too often or if the solution is too strong. Squashing aphids with your fingers is another way to remove an early infestation but can get messy if a large colony has built up.

STREAKS AND SPOTS

Pale green and yellow streaks on the leaves or striped patterns on the petals are a sign of virus. In extreme cases, the virus weakens and distorts the plant. It may survive for many years but is rarely attractive – the exception being some of the fabled 'broken' tulips that can have wonderful patterns on the flowers. Virus is spread by aphids as they move from one plant to another. Vigorous plants may be healthy enough to carry virus without succumbing to its effects, and seeds do not carry the virus so you can try growing new plants.

Rusts are a fungal infection made visible by their coloured, spore-producing bodies called pustules, often seen on the leaves. Healthy plants will pull through but make sure you dispose of infected leaves. Use fungicides to treat bad outbreaks.

BULB-SPECIFIC PESTS

Narcissus bulb fly can kill daffodils and other plants in the same family, such as snowdrops and nerines. The fly lays an egg on the neck of the plant and, once hatched, the maggot crawls down to the bulb and eats it from the inside out. Firm the soil around bulbs after flowering, to deter narcissus bulb fly.

Lily beetle attacks lilies and other bulbs in the family, such as fritillaries. Bright red beetles can be seen in summer but fall to the ground when disturbed, exposing their dark undersides and making them very difficult to find. You must be quick to squash them. Their larvae eat the leaves, leaving excrement all over them.

Tulip fire is a fungal disease that can devastate a tulip collection. Thriving in humid conditions, it starts with blotches on the flower and leaves, spreading to cause severe marking and distortion before killing the bulb. A bright, sunny position, with plenty of air movement, reduces the likelihood of tulip fire spreading. If you do have it, remove all tulips close by and grow something else for at least three years.

What to do when

AUTUMN

Preparing

- For many garden bulbs, autumn is the beginning of the year, so plan what bulbs you want and where to plant them. If you have not done already, buy bulbs now. The earlier you start the more choice you will have, as popular varieties sell out.
- Cut back herbaceous perennials to make room for bulb planting in borders.
- Dig over the soil, adding organic matter if necessary, to improve drainage and provide nutrients (see Soil preparation and planting, page 18).
- As summer containers begin to fade, tip out the plants and clean each pot, ready for new soil and spring bulbs.

Growing

- Plant winter and spring bulbs in the garden or in containers. Early autumn is a good time for most bulbs (see Designing a spring bulb extravaganza, page 86), but some such as tulips can wait until later in the season. Lilies are often sold in spring but, if you can get them early, plant them now.
- Remember that for most bulbs deeper planting is better, so use a good, strong trowel to dig holes for larger bulbs.
- Collect seed from summer-flowering bulbs if you want to grow more and keep them cool and dry until ready to sow (see Growing bulbs from seed, page 104).

Maintaining

- Cut back the dry stems of summer bulbs.
- Weed the garden and clear away fallen leaves from autumn-flowering bulbs, to show them off at their best.
- Mulch your borders in late autumn, with garden compost, leafmould or well-rotted manure. This provides nutrients for the bulbs and keeps weeds down and moisture in the soil. Use gravel in a dry garden or rock garden.
- Bring pots of half-hardy bulbs undercover, to protect them from frost.

WINTER

Preparing

- Keeping the garden tidy is easy at this time of year, as weeds grow very slowly, if at all, and most tree leaves will have blown away or been cleared already. It is still worth looking around occasionally, to make sure any early bulbs such as snowdrops (*Galanthus*) and winter aconite (*Eranthis hyemalis*) are not smothered.
- If temperatures below −5°C/23°F are forecast, give some extra protection to the less hardy plants such as African lily (*Agapanthus*). Cover their crowns with leaves or horticultural fleece, until the weather improves.

Growing

- Winter is also the time to sow seed so sow those of hardy bulbs, whether autumn-, spring- or summer-flowering (see Growing bulbs from seed, page 104). Many need a cold spell before they germinate, so leave

Autumn is the time to plant winter- and spring-flowering bulbs.

Ensure bulbs such as winter aconite (*Eranthis hyemalis*) are not smothered by fallen leaves.

them outside to get that winter chill. Once the seedlings appear, protect them from the coldest weather.

- If the soil is not frozen, plant hardy summer bulbs such as lilies and montbretia (*Crocosmia*) towards the end of winter.
- After snowdrops (*Galanthus*) have flowered, they can be lifted and divided. Spread them around and open up any dense clumps, to improve flowering the following year.
- Buy snowdrops 'in the green' and plant them as soon as you can (see Planting a winter bulb garden, page 120).

Maintaining
- Most bulbs will be in full growth by now so regularly check pots kept in a greenhouse or conservatory, on a windowsill, even those outside, as in a dry spell they can dry out and so need water.

- Clear away any remaining tree leaves so that winter bulbs are free to flower.
- If you grow summer bulbs permanently in pots, now is a good time to repot them (see Growing bulbs in pots, page 20). Tip them out and clean the pot thoroughly to prevent any diseases spreading. Always use fresh new soil mix to replant the bulbs.

SPRING
Preparing
- As the weather warms and the days lengthen, the garden bursts into life. Flowers can come and go quickly, from crocuses and daffodils (*Narcissus*), to tulips and ornamental onions (*Allium*). Soak it all in and make the most of sunny days. Make a note of anything you want to change; if something is perfect, take note of that too. Take photographs and visit other gardens for ideas.

- After they have flowered, it is important to keep the bulbs growing as long as possible, as they need to build up strength to come back next year.

Growing
- Sow seed of less hardy bulbs (see Growing bulbs from seed, page 104) and protect them from any late frosts. If you have a cold frame or greenhouse, keep the seed pots in there and do not forget to water them; they can dry out quickly on a warm spring day.
- Continue to plant summer bulbs, especially those that are less hardy such as African lily (*Agapanthus*), foxtail lily (*Eremurus*), pineapple lily (*Eucomis*) and gladiolus.
- Squash aphids as they start to appear or treat with soapy water or insecticide (see Distorted growth, page 136). Early treatment will prevent an uncontrollable infestation.

Maintaining
- Water pots and window boxes regularly as they can dry out surprisingly quickly, but do not overdo it; check the soil below the immediate surface to see if it is dry.
- Keep on top of weeds, which will start to grow now, to prevent them getting out of hand.
- Look out for signs of virus or fungal diseases (see Troubleshooting, page 137). If a plant is badly affected, it is wise to remove it completely and dispose of it. Do not put diseased plants in the garden compost,

because viruses and fungal disease can spread this way.
- Feed bulbs that look like they need a boost, both in the garden and in pots. Sprinkle low-nitrogen fertilizer on the soil and let the rain water it in, or use a liquid feed.
- As bulbs finish flowering, allow the leaves to continue growing. Water them if they need it, especially those in pots, and do not remove the leaves before they have gone brown. Check for seeds if you want to collect them.
- Do not cut the grass if you have bulbs growing in a lawn. Wait at least six weeks after they have flowered to allow them to die down naturally.
- Lift and divide bulbs as they die down, while you can see where they are. Replant them straightaway and water them in so they can keep growing as much as possible (see Simple propagation, page 23).

SUMMER
Preparing
- Keep taking note of any good plant combinations or gaps that need filling. Summer bulbs have to compete with an array of summer flowers so if you have created a beautiful mix make sure you can remember it; photograph it, write it down and, above all, enjoy it.
- The first catalogues and bulb lists will start to appear now and you can begin planning next year's display. If there are particular bulbs you want to grow, order them early.

LEFT African lily (*Agapanthus*) can make a glorious summer display.

ABOVE When the bulb flowers have faded and their stems have dried out, they can be carefully removed to keep the garden tidy.

Growing

- Plant autumn bulbs such as meadow saffron (*Colchicum*) and cyclamen (see Naturalizing autumn bulbs in your garden, page 114). They will flower as soon as there is a hint of autumn in the air so you do not want to leave them out of the ground for too long.
- Late summer is a good time to propagate bulbs. Try bulb scoring, chipping or twin-scaling, using some spare spring bulbs (see Simple propagation, page 23). By the next spring you may have produced many more bulbs.
- If you have seedlings that have been in their pot a year or more, tip them out when dormant to see how the little bulbs are doing. If large enough, plant them in a bigger pot for another year.

Maintaining

- In early summer you can start cutting the grass where late-spring bulbs were growing. The cut area will look untidy and brown at first but the grass soon recovers.
- Clear away the dead leaves of spring bulbs so they do not sit on the ground and rot away. The fungal spores can spread to other plants.
- Look out for lily beetles and remove them as soon as they appear (see Bulb-specific pests, page 137).
- Keep weeding the garden to keep it tidy and to prevent the weeds competing with the plants you do want to thrive.
- Water pots regularly and check the garden soil, too. A long, dry spell can be damaging for summer bulbs.
- Cut back the seed heads of ornamental onions (*Allium*) once they begin to look untidy. Some may have seeds so collect them if you want to try growing them or allow them to fall naturally and germinate in the border.

Index

Brimming with creative inspiration, how-to projects and useful information to enrich your everyday life, Quarto Knows is a favourite destination for those pursuing their interests and passions. Visit our site and dig deeper with our books into your area of interest: Quarto Creates, Quarto Cooks, Quarto Homes, Quarto Lives, Quarto Drives, Quarto Explores, Quarto Gifts, or Quarto Kids.

First published in 2019 by White Lion Publishing, an imprint of The Quarto Group.
The Old Brewery, 6 Blundell Street
London, N7 9BH,
United Kingdom
T (0)20 7700 6700 F (0)20 7700 8066
www.QuartoKnows.com

Text © 2019 Richard Wilford
Illustrations © the Board of Trustees
of the Royal Botanic Gardens, Kew

A catalogue record for this book is available from the British Library.

ISBN 978-0-7112-3934-0

10 9 8 7 6 5 4

Typeset in Stempel Garamond and Univers
Design by Sarah Pyke

Printed in China

Photographic acknowledgements
a=above; b=below; m=middle; l=left; r=right

© **Jason Ingram** 18m+b, 35al+am+ar, 51al+am+ar+bl, 59al+am+ar+bl, 71al+ar+ml+mr, 79al+ar+bl, 105al+am+ar+ml, 121al, 141r

© **Richard Wilford** 8, 11, 13l+r, 13r, 15, 17, 20, 21r, 25al+ar+b, 35bl+br, 37, 39, 41, 44, 46a, 47a, 64, 71b, 79ml+br, 83, 87am+ar+br, 105mr+b, 113, 115al+ar+b, 121am+bl+br, 122, 129al+am+ar+bl+br, 133, 134, 135

© **Shutterstock** 2 Denys Dolnikov, 6–7 Natasha Breen, 13 Cornelia Pithart, 18t bluedog studio, 21l Natalia van D, 22 Martin Fowler, 26–7 EsHanPhot, 28 RukiMedia, 29 Martina Kieselbach, 30 Martin Fowler, 32 Flower_Garden, 36 Heiti Paves, 40 Sarah Marhant, 43 Sarycheva Olesia, 45 Peter Turner Photography, 46b catus, 47b Jordan Tan, 48 Sinelev, 49 Przemyslaw Muszynski, 51br RukiMedia, 52 Del Boy, 53 RukiMedia, 54 Peter_Fleming, 55 RaGS2, 56 Natalia van D, 57 Victoria Kurylo, 59br Peter Turner Photography, 61 Linda George, 62 Natalia van D, 63 Frauke Ross, 65 Annaev, 66 Predrag Lukic, 67 Del Boy, 68 Cristian Gusa, 69 Andrew Fletcher, 72 Gucio_55, 73 Haidamac, 74 Ruth Swan, 75 Peter Turner Photography, 76 Hivaka, 77 Ihor Martsenyuk, 79mr Flower_Garden, 80 Gabriela Beres, 81 ajisai13, 82 acchity, 84 Bob Saunders, 85 alybaba, 87al Drozdowski, 87bl J Need, 88 Mihai-Bogdan Lazar, 89 padu-foto, 90 Nick Pecker, 91 Gherzak, 92 Jiang Tianmu, 93 Guillermo Guerao Serra, 95al+r Polina Lobanova, 95ml rob3rt82, 95bl Aleksei Verhovski, 95br Rozova Svetlana, 96 Itija, 97 V J Matthew, 98 rontav, 99l Nick Pecker, 99r sebastianosecondi, 101 Oxik, 103 Peter Turner Photography, 106 art of line, 107 Fenneke Smouter, 108 Tamara Kulikova, 109 Matt Hopkins, 110 mizy, 112 Julian Popov, 116 Byron Ortiz, 117 Brian A Wolf, 118 RukiMedia, 119 Sheila Fitzgerald, 121ar Ernie Janes, 123 J Need, 124 Skysprayer2005, 125 NataliaVo, 126 Peter_Fleming, 127 Janelle Lugge, 130 Madelein Molfaardt, 131 Zigzag Mountain Art, 132 Doikanoy, 137 L.A. Faille, 139l OlgaPonomarenko, 139r Jgade, 141l ingehogenbijl